ANASTASIA PETRENKO

BE YOUR OWN GURU

34 ESSAYS ON FIGURING OUT LIFE

Copyright © 2023 Anastasia Petrenko
All rights reserved.

No part of this publication may be reproduced, distributed, or transmitted in any form or by any means, including photocopying, recording, or other electronic or mechanical methods, without the prior written permission of the author. For permission requests, contact contact@anastasiawhy.com.

Cover design: Anastasia Volodchenkova

ISBN: 978-1-7389810-3-8

CONTENTS

INTRODUCTION 8

EXPECTING EXPECTATIONS 14

ATTENDING ATTENTION 22

QUESTIONING QUESTIONS 34

COMMUNICATING COMMUNICATION 40

HEARING TO LISTEN 46

THE IMPORTANCE OF YOUR SENSE OF IMPORTANCE .. 52

A NARRATIVE ABOUT NARRATIVES 58

MAKING A CHOICE ABOUT MAKING A CHOICE 66

CARING ABOUT CARE 76

RESOLVING CONTRADICTIONS 84

DESERVING YOUR VALUE 90

INNER MONOLOGUES 96

LIVING IN THE PRESENT 102

FILLING UP EMPTINESS	110
IMPATIENT ABOUT PATIENCE	118
THE PATH OF PERFECTION	124
JUDGING PREJUDGEMENTS	132
AUTHENTICALLY ABOUT AUTHENTICITY	138
ACCUSING EXCUSES	144
DISAPPROVING APPROVAL	150
ON MEDIA NOISE	156
VALUING VALUE	162
SABOTAGING SELF-SABOTAGE	174
PRIORITIZING PRIORITIZATION	184
ACTING ON ACTIONS	194
GRATIFYING GRATITUDE	204
TRY TRYING	212
LAZILY ABOUT LAZINESS	220
UNBORING BOREDOM	228
RESPECTING SELF-RESPECT	240

PROMISING PROMISES	250
ACCEPTING REJECTION	256
REGRETTING REGRET	266
INFINITY ON OUR FINITUDE, OR MEMENTO MORI	276
INSTEAD OF AN AFTERWORD	284
NOTES	286
ABOUT THE AUTHOR	289

To everyone who is feeling lost at sea.

INTRODUCTION

INTRODUCTION

A child's relationship with the world is naturally based on the basic components of "school," "toys," "candy," and "mom." As time passes, abstract concepts are added — "pain," "hurt," "joy," "love," — and life gets more complicated. And when gradations join the vocabulary party — "lovely," "awkward," "ideal," "annoying," — nothing ever seems clear or straightforward from here on out.

As we grow up, life becomes more challenging and confusing. The more we expand our vocabulary and accumulate experiences, the more we get lost in ourselves and the world around us. "White lies," "broken heart," "ultimate success," "unfulfilling life" — these lexical creations introduce a frenzy to our already puzzled emotional states.

With the enormous flow of information and the relentless number of decisions that bombard us daily, it's no wonder we don't examine each idea and each feeling we have carefully. We don't give much thought to the concepts that are already ingrained in our speech, such as "regret," "choice," and "value," that we use superficially. We swallow the terms that pop psychology generously supplies, such as "untapped potential," "core values," and "self-care," without digesting them; that is, without ever truly knowing what they mean to us.

Moreover, we accept them gladly because they promise us a better future, and deep down, or on the surface of our psyche, we all believe that we can be better and have it better. We *deserve* better. But ask us what exactly this *better* is or what we've done to deserve it and it suddenly loses its appeal and lightness.

Should we proceed toward our *better*, we need to examine our realities of the present, our ideas of the future, and question what *good* and *good enough* is for us; terms that are not nearly as sexy as "untapped potential" or "powerful vulnerability" (but they are more important for going forward).

When we blindly follow self-help advice, we may believe we chart our own path toward a better life, but what we are really doing is placing ourselves into the cultural stencil. While some shared wisdom provides valid shortcuts to our well-being, some revelations have to be made on our own, lest we risk being lost forever.

I invite you to examine the common concepts you encounter in your daily life with greater scrutiny. What do "attention," "gratitude," and "authenticity" mean to you? The fact that there is a word to describe a quality, state, or feeling means humankind finds them significant enough to name them. And even if the descriptions are imperfect, they provide good starting points for unraveling our struggles. *What causes self-sabotage? Why do we believe in merit? How is patience a virtue given our limited lifespan?* Using my reading background, personal experience, and restless curiosity, I explore the key concepts that can improve our lives and invite you to join me.

That being said, I don't claim to know what is right for you. I don't know better — only you know what is right for you. All I am offering is food for thought paired with questions that have the potential to change your actions, and therefore your life, for the better. But how this *better* looks for you, you decide.

INTRODUCTION

All views and ponderings contained within this book are not dogma or truth in the last resort. They are an invitation to dialogue that will help you gain a deeper understanding of yourself and this life. I'm not teaching you. I'm not telling you how to live and who to be. You are who you are and the life you live is yours, unique and unrepeatable. With this book, I simply encourage you to delve into your experience of living and, if you're willing, improve it.

Maybe you finally take a hiatus and self-reflect, maybe you finally cull bad ideas that impede your self-fulfillment, or maybe you just finally define what self-fulfillment is for you and reevaluate your beliefs. You can't expect any book to catapult you into "perfect life" enlightenment, but you can expect to find a heaping helping of hope that you are okay and can always improve. That the problems you are currently facing have solutions, that the beliefs you're holding onto can be calibrated to better serve you. That your mind, which quite willingly supplies various distortions, can also keep the truth upfront in your daily consciousness so you have fewer loopholes and excuses to succumb to misery. It will, however, take some hard work: you'll need to move past mental agoraphobia and embrace the world of possibilities that this experience of being alive offers.

My goal is not to please you or gain your approval. Quite the contrary in fact. If my written lines provoke a strong emotional reaction in you, particularly dissatisfaction and anger, then you'll be more likely to recall what you've read and draw your own conclusions, conclusions you're less likely to forget, regardless of whether they agree or contradict mine. What matters most is that they are meaningful to you and make your life worthwhile.

I wrote this book as a letter to friends to support them through the struggles we all face, while also giving them a safe space to express themselves. If you'd like to share your story, you're more than welcome to send me a message (my contact information can be found at the end of the book).

In this book, I use "we" more often than "you" because although your life is unique, we all share similar fears and experience similar feelings. We make mistakes and compile regrets. We want to improve but often fall short. And even though your journey is unparalleled with mine, or with those of eight billion other humans, we are all subject to primal instincts and hormonal regulations. While we haven't yet understood explicitly all our biochemistry and its influence on our decision-making and moods, we can witness the results of our actions and use that data to alter our future behavior in a way where it'll be more beneficial to our well-being. Simply put, we can learn by reflecting on our own experiences as well as those of others.

One last note before we set sail: as you read this book, you will come to see how closely related the chapters are, and how one term will serve as a building block for understanding another concept. Feel free to navigate this book as you would Wikipedia: follow your curiosity to make sense of complex

INTRODUCTION

subjects by breaking them down to their essential components. Each chapter contains questions that I hope you'll take a moment to consider as well as one or two concrete practices that can help you improve the aspect of your life discussed. And perhaps the insights you gain will lead you to a happier if not more meaningful life. And I'd argue that the latest is far more precious.

Thanks for trusting me with your time. Now let's get started.

EXPECTING EXPECTATIONS

expectation (n)

a strong belief that something will happen or be the case
- *disappointment is nothing more than dashed expectations.*

a belief that someone will or should achieve something
- *we have high expectations of our people and our partners.*

EXPECTING EXPECTATIONS

Dreams and wishes that don't come true are always disappointments. And disappointments, as we have all very much experienced, are a source of pain. «I was supposed to get that promotion!» «I had planned to be on the beach by now, not stuck in this snowstorm!» «I thought she would never leave me!» Yet, we don't nip the potential frustrations in the bud. On the contrary, we cultivate them. We keep envisioning that life will turn out as we want and plan, leaving a small space for a chance.

> *Expectations were like fine pottery. The harder you held them, the more likely they were to crack.*
>
> Brandon Sanderson

One of the reasons we act like masochists is because reality's harshness helps us grow. We may not like this fact, but we know it's true. And who among us doesn't want to become a better version of ourselves? It is only through challenge and defeat that we can change our behavior to learn more, know better, and potentially reap greater self-fulfilling rewards. This idea is perfectly summarized by the «no pain, no gain» cliché. I trust your life path has proven it to be true.

But what about a self-destructive manner of wanting and wishing that doesn't bring anything except disapntments? There are obvious ways to guarantee you will feel miserable, such as wishing to own a material item that is far beyond your budget and common sense (With-

> **Expectations are resentments waiting to happen.**
>
> Anne Lamott

out this 100-*foot yacht, I've failed in my life!*), or your dream of not working yet having "passive income" flow into your bank account (*I don't want to be stressed running my own business, but I do want a seven-figure passive income!*).

And then there are the subtle and more dangerous ways to become vexed, such as wanting others to behave as you want them to, expecting them to see the world as you see it and believing they understand you as much as you understand yourself. That's a recipe for perpetual grumpiness.

"I've been working overtime for months but my boss doesn't promote me!"

"I made it clear to him that I wanted that dress. Still, he hasn't bought it for me for my birthday!"

"She should always want sex as much as I do!"

"They could at least invite us over for dinner after all the charity work we've done for them!"

"I wish she stopped being resentful because of that stupid dress!"

We are spiteful creatures. It's easy for us to find reasons to complain, yet it takes conscious effort to be grateful. It's easy for us to be discontented with our lives and it takes some harsh events to make us fall in love with our existence again.

EXPECTING EXPECTATIONS

What's worse is how deeply and naturally planted our tendency is to form certain expectations of other people, how pervasive this propensity is. Yet it's impossible to live without any — our past experiences help us navigate the present. There are, however, adequate expectations like *"a pizza guy delivers a pizza to me,"* and inadequate ones like *"my boyfriend must buy me a new iPhone."*

The majority of our inadequate expectations come from the media and society: physical beauty standards of fashion and Instagram models that are impossible to reach, perfect lives displayed through carefully curated social media posts by famous people and our acquaintances, and success stories of the few that make it look easy and fast. In most cases, these expectations are crushed by reality. We don't become star athletes or supermodels just because we wished to be. Our romantic partners aren't always smiles and sunshine. We don't have rapid career growth as we see it in movies or read about in selectively crafted bios. We understand how unrealistic the world of media is and yet we let it influence our minds, self-esteem, and mood.

It's reasonable to stop having expectations that prove to be unsustainable. I know it's easier said than done, but if we're serious about our intentions to have better days, moods, and relationships, we can find a way. There's always a way.

Here are two things that worked for me:

- Be mindful of the phrase *"I wish you/he/she/they..."* When I catch myself having these thoughts, I cut them off and dis-

> **The quality of our expectations determines the quality of our action.**
>
> Jean-Baptiste Andre Godin

card them as invalid. The conclusions they lead to will be wrong, since the premise they are based on is wrong, so what's the point of dwelling on them? Practice makes it easier to recognize such pernicious thoughts and ignore them.

- Accompany *"must"* with *"why."* When I see I have expectations of other people, I prefer to make sure they are grounded and are not just my whims. I break the dogmatic circle of certain expectations by asking *why?* questions. Why do I expect him/her/them to act in certain ways? What are the grounds for such thinking? Did we exchange marriage vows, sign a contract, or make a pinky swear? Are these grounds valid? By answering these questions I learn how poorly I reason and how unfounded most of my expectations are.

But it's important to remember that this practice is no cakewalk. It does, however, decrease the number of disappointments and helps to avoid unneeded frustrations. If you give it a try, you may even shift your whole attitude about daily interactions, especially with strangers, making space for pleasant surprises.

When you embrace the reality that no one owes you anything, each action of other people, and yours, becomes more meaningful. Have someone let you cut in line? Listened to your story? Helped you figure out parking? They didn't have to do these kind deeds, yet they did. Showing more gratitude and less entitlement can make a big difference. It can help you become more self-reliant and kinder, and make others' days brighter and more pleasant.

When it comes to those closest to us, we can't have no expectations. That would be unrealistic and, frankly, wrong. After all, we are bound to those particular people by ties that make our relationships meaningful. The same practice outlined above — stopping "*I wish they...*" thoughts and questioning the reasons behind your expectations — will improve the quality of your dear relationships. Recognizing the efforts of your loved ones and letting them know you appreciate their contribution to your well-being will prevent the build-up of resentment. No one likes being taken for granted and you can be the first to show what it's like to be grateful.

When we stop waiting for others to act the way we want them to act, we grow as individuals. It's not about lowering our expectations; it's about making them reasonable.

We reduce day-to-day drama. We decrease the pain in our life. We fortify our character.

So let's give it a try.

WRITE DOWN YOUR

three expectations that did come true:

_____

_____

_____

two expectations that didn't come true:

_____

_____

Were these expectations about you, other people, or circumstances?

_____

_____

Write down an expectation that you currently have:

_____

_____

Who bears the brunt of making this expectation come true*?

_____

_____

*If it's not you, consider how you can either take responsibility for it or remove this expectation to avoid disappointment.

ATTENDING
ATTENTION

attention (n)

the mental faculty of considering or taking notice of someone or something

- *he turned his attention to the educational system.*

the action of dealing with or taking special care of someone or something

- *her business needed her attention.*

ATTENDING ATTENTION

Every second, we receive 11 million bits of information from our environment.¹ Our conscious minds, however, can only process 50 bits of it (that is 0.00045455%, a mere ten-thousandth of the total). While we miss out on much of what exists, what remains can feel overwhelming. Kids are screaming, phones are vibrating, and the car on the right is cutting us off. In such a maelstrom of stimuli it's easy to get dizzy or irritated, let alone to stay focused. But we manage. We prioritize safety and despite chaos and traffic, we maintain our concentration and get to our destination alive.

Our attention evolved to facilitate us to initiate motor commands in response to changes in our environment. If we see danger, we react: run, freeze, or hit the brakes, thus increasing our chances of survival. But motor responses are not enough to stay functional in our society. We should also stay alert so we don't make serious mistakes at work that could get us fired. If we're not present, the quality of our lives deteriorates.

> *Where attention goes, energy flows and results show.*
> T. Harv Eker

Attention is a life-creating tool. Sadly, we are often inept at handling it. We don't know how to retain focus and make the most of it. We go along with habit and distraction. From an evolutionary lens, this has its advantages: habits preserve our mental resources and distractions allow us to perceive potentially harmful and beneficial elements in the environment.

A distraction is, of course, anything that captures our attention without our consent. We are all too familiar with the situation when we try to concentrate on the task at hand but then switch to listening to our colleagues because they might talk about us or something else important, or picking up our phone because we're bored and looking for a dose of dopamine. All of this, voluntary and involuntary attention, makes up our lives.

Attention is the filter for our consciousness. It sifts out what we think we don't need, paints a negative picture of what we fear, and gives priority to what we enjoy. The problem is that we apply this filter habitually and universally, even where it might not work properly, leading to omissions and distortions; from small oversights (we didn't look at our plate and chew on someone else's hair) to major ones (we didn't notice the change in our loved one's behavior and then become dumbstruck when asked for a divorce). Or how about the times when we feared public speaking, imagined how it would go wrong rather than getting prepared and motivated by seeing the opportunities the speech offers?

ATTENDING ATTENTION

Being inattentive can be costly, just as being attentive to the wrong things. We pay attention to a person's clothing brand and miss key information in their words; we think of what to make for dinner and fail to notice that we've been shortchanged; we turn to our phone's notifications and miss a change in traffic lights.

> *Attention is the mother of memory.*
>
> Unknown

More than ever before, we live in a time rich in experience and knowledge. Internet access and the sophistication of the entertainment industry make our lives exciting. But because of our mental constraints that can't handle the vast volume of data we receive, we become more and more accustomed to absorbing information superficially — skimming articles, listening to podcasts half-heartedly, and "watching" videos while reading comments.

This habit of superficial information consumption saves mental energy. We don't need to watch every pixel of a kitten video to appreciate its cuteness, just as we don't need to read every word of the article on tax increases to find out what the new rate is. But this approach can also be a time-waster — we spent time looking for answers but we missed them so we have to revisit the material.

By taking information hastily, we also rob ourselves of potential excitement and eye-opening knowledge. We miss almost everything surrounding us when we lack focus, leading to a woeful paucity, to a two-dimensional existence. As we walk, we're too caught up in our thoughts to notice a baby squirrel trying to handle a nut bigger than its head, or as we scroll social media and read a phrase only to forget it a second later. We waste time and gain nothing in return. The good news is that if we can learn to orchestrate our attention, the next time we stop to read a phrase we can remember it and let it enrich our thinking.

The ability to consciously redirect and retain attention is one of our greatest powers. If we want to achieve outstanding results, learn a new skill, or remember a sweet moment, we need our attention spotlighting the right spot — not an interlocutor's jacket brand but their words, not casual discussions of coworkers but our task at hand, not our social media feed but traffic.

If you can listen attentively to others, they'll want to talk to you. If you can work thoughtfully, you avoid mistakes and help others prevent them, and they'll want to cooperate with you further. If we're so thoroughly immersed in our reality of the here and now, we can achieve exceptional results in anything we do.

So how do you learn to get out of autopilot and dive into the essence of your "now"? One of the most effective exercises to flex your attention muscle is meditation. We've all

ATTENDING ATTENTION

heard that meditation is about being aware of the present, to be in the moment. Although awareness and attention are not the same — awareness is like peripheral vision while attention is like central — being observant helps you move out of autopilot mode and into the present. When you practice mindfulness by noticing what's going on around you and how you feel in the moment, you learn to take control of your fleeting attention, if only for a few seconds at a time before it slips away again. The more you practice, the more often and quickly you can recognize when you are lost in the whirlpool of your thoughts and switch to what you consider more important.

Another effective way to learn to manage your attention is by intentionally looking for things you haven't paid attention to before. Let's say you usually check the expiration date of a product at the supermarket. Next time you go to the store, look at its ingredients, its nutritional value, or where the product was made. This intentional redirection to new information is an easy activity and sometimes all you need to do is to move your eyes. When going on your walk, you can glance up and see which lampposts lack bulbs or lower your gaze and see where the grass bursts through concrete cracks. Or you can close your eyes and hear affluence sounds you didn't know were there.

By focusing on the things you previously ignored, not only will you learn to direct your attention better, but you will also gain the ability to see the bigger picture and, when faced

> *Attention is the sculptor that shapes our reality.*
>
> Unknown

with problems, will be able to come up with more creative and effective solutions. This practice can also develop an appreciation for ordinary things. A light bulb may be nothing remarkable to you, yet if you look carefully, you'll give it significance and recognize how it makes your life easier.

Also, make sure you don't compromise your concentration. Do you have a phone on your desk and dozens of tabs open in your browser? They are barriers to what is already a challenging task — paying attention. If you want to assist in your goal of staying focused, you need to remove distractions. Put your phone away, limit the number of websites opened, and close the door if you have one; these simple actions will help you achieve a state of flow.

Another thing you might want to look at is your habit of scrolling and multitasking. By engaging in such activities, you become less capable of concentrating consciously on one task at a time. We've gotten used to creating the illusion of multitasking: working while listening to a podcast, watching a movie while discussing the news, driving while talking on the phone. And although

ATTENDING ATTENTION

we can process information coming from different senses at once, its quality suffers and our performance drops. To achieve above-average results in whatever you do, you need to overcome this harmful habit of chasing multiple irritants.

You can train yourself to focus on one thing by reading ordinary paper books. They have no pop-up banners, no ramiparous paths across the web, and no likes and comments under each page. If you get bored or struggle to read a chapter without getting distracted by your phone and getting lost in the mazes of irrelevant thoughts, then this practice can definitely benefit you. Start with one page but read it mindfully so you can summarize what you've just learned.

Using the practices outlined here, you'll start experiencing fatigue, which is completely normal. Being attentive takes up a lot of energy. At most, our brain is capable of staying focused for up to two hours, and then it needs a break. If we don't give it detente, it'll make it for itself. No matter what we do, no matter how hard we grasp the steering wheel of our consciousness, we'll be thrown back in the passenger seat hundreds of times throughout the day. But exercising our attention muscle prepares us to get behind the wheel quickly and skillfully whenever a sharp turn comes up, or an accident might occur, or if we wish to take a less comfortable but more scenic route. Figuratively and literally speaking.

Being attentive also helps you understand yourself better. What you pay attention to can tell you a lot about who you are, what your values are, and what drives you. Maybe you think too much about meals or grudges, which prevents you from doing quality work and having healthy relationships, and not enough about how you can solve recurring problems, and help others and yourself. Try to notice the repeated themes in your thinking and behavior and consider whether they broadcast the kind of person you want to be. There is still a difference between someone who listens to their conversation partner or thinks about dessert, someone who focuses on the news about the Kardashians or about NASA. When we're simultaneously bombarded with multiple bits of information (which is always), how we discriminate among them tells others and ourselves what we find important and therefore, with whom we can bond, cooperate, and be happier.

Being attentive to oneself opens up a dimension of meta attentiveness; that is, paying attention to what we pay attention to. Most of us, by default, see problems rather than opportunities. We focus on the negatives rather than the positives, and we judge others' missteps rather than take responsibility for our own. But when we are mindful, we can avoid falling victim to our weaknesses, such as being fearful, pessimistic, and judgemental, and redirect our attention to more rewarding experiences such as appreciating nature, stories of loved ones, and our ability to think.

We all have different lives, accomplishments, and levels of life satisfaction, not just because of our innate qualities and random circumstances but because of how we direct our attention. With the ability to choose what we focus on, we're much better equipped to have exceptional lives with fewer regrets and more wonders.

WRITE DOWN

three things you pay attention to daily:

_____

_____

_____

three things you want to pay better attention to:

_____

_____

_____

Why do you pay attention to the first three things, and what stops you from paying attention to the other three?

_____
_____
_____
_____
_____
_____

QUESTIONING QUESTIONS

question (n)

a sentence worded or expressed so as to elicit information

- *we hope this leaflet has been helpful in answering your questions.*

the raising of a doubt about or objection to something

- *her loyalty is beyond question*

a matter requiring resolution or discussion

- *the biggest question facing our society today is how we can create a more equitable and just world for all.*

Questions are critical components of our development. No progress can be made without asking questions.

Do you remember how curious you were as a child? Your endless line of questions baffled your parents, probably even annoyed them. But you were persistent and kept asking. Why is the sky blue? Do monkeys only eat bananas? What does WiFi stand for? Where do thoughts come from? And babies? You had to figure out that mashed-up world and your part in it.

When we grow up, however, we tend to become arrogant, believing that we know the answers. We get assertive, stop questioning the answers we have, and we get less curious, asking fewer and fewer questions. Or worse, we lose interest in asking questions altogether and stop participating in life.

You and I, we're both aware we can't know everything. Life is so tricky that we can't even be sure about what we think we know. It doesn't mean, however, that we should give up on knowledge and stop exploring. For that very reason, that life is uncertain and full of mysteries, we should keep exploring it. The best way to do this is to ask questions. But

> *The important thing is not to stop questioning. Curiosity has its own reason for existence.*
>
> Albert Einstein

> **The art and science of asking questions is the source of all knowledge.**
>
> Thomas Berger

it's not as simple as it seems. Just putting a question mark at the end won't do.

Asking questions is an art. The answers we receive depend on what and how we ask. A properly posed question brings the truth closer. An ambiguous question pushes it away. We often ask a simple question "What?" which presupposes a self-evident answer, rather than a puzzling question "Why?" which doesn't offer such a univocity. A question with an obvious answer doesn't do much for our self-development whereas an open question has the potential to reveal mind-boggling ideas and, thus, expand our frameworks of thought.

Asking the right questions is a mentally consuming process. It requires us to be assiduous — have you noticed how often we settle for the first offered answer? — and humble. We must admit ignorance and be open to hearing an answer, no matter how unpleasant or shocking. But if done correctly, we learn regardless of whether or not we receive answers. Posing the right questions makes even silence eloquent.

Isn't this a key part of our existence, to learn and experience what it's like to be alive? We don't know what we discover along the way but the beauty of discovering is what makes life exciting.

Questions are doorways to the unknown where your life happens. Do you have the courage to go through them?

> *We make our world significant by the courage of our questions and by the depth of our answers.*
>
> Carl Sagan

WRITE DOWN

a question that makes you uncomfortable and that you've been avoiding asking yourself:

___

a question that you always wanted to ask someone close to you, but never did:

___

you wish someone close to you had asked you:

___

you can't find an answer to:

___

you regret not asking:

_____

Are these questions formulated in a way that will provide the most clarity and understanding when answered?

_____

COMMUNICATING COMMUNICATION

communication (n)

the imparting or exchanging of information by speaking, writing, or using some other medium

- *writing is an effective means of communication.*
- *the only way he communicates with me is through text messages.*

the successful conveying or sharing of ideas and feelings

- *words and how we use them can make or break our ability to communicate effectively.*

Our ancestors' survival depended largely on their ability to adapt and communicate. Those who could adjust to changing conditions left offspring, as we all know. But what role did communication play and why is it still so crucial to our viability?

Unless our predecessors could share information, they wouldn't be able to warn each other about impending threats, and thus, they wouldn't be able to avoid or prepare for them. Unless they could share information, we'd have to risk our own lives in order to learn what a cure is and what foods are poisonous. Unless our ancestors communicated their knowledge, we wouldn't have electricity, heating, water purification, and the omnipresent Internet!

Undoubtedly, communication brings us a lot of good. But if done poorly, it can be misleading, harmful, or even life-threatening. Numerous tragedies have resulted from inadequate communication: the collapse of the walkway at the Hyatt Regency, the Fukushima Daiichi nuclear disaster, the Piper Bravo rig explosion, and the consequences of the Chornobyl meltdown to name a few. For a glimpse of poor communication verbatim, look up the transcript of the deadliest avia-

> *The single biggest problem in communication is the illusion that it has taken place.*
>
> George Bernard Shaw

> **Communication works for those who work at it.**
>
> John Powell

tion accident in history — The Tenerife Airport disaster.

Communication is an equation with many variables: a sender, a recipient, a channel, and a message. Just one component malfunctions, just one false move, and we deal with erroneous conclusions and decisions. Look at our lives: every minute of every day we transmit and receive information. And every minute of everyday disruptions happen. We may misinterpret another person's message, or we may not be clear in our own messages. As a result of these misunderstandings, we create grudges, make costly mistakes, and fail to achieve our goals.

To reduce the interference, we need to be humble and accept the bitter truth: we are lazy communicators. We often talk carelessly, read absent-mindedly, and answer hurriedly. Additionally, we are rarely well-informed, and most of the time we don't have reliable sources. As if that were not enough, we also have biases and prejudices that affect how we process information. Only when we accept these unflattering facts, can we hear and, most importantly, listen to each other.

Mastering our thoughts is another critical component of eliminating breaches. When we think clearly, we express our thoughts clearly, resulting in more precise communication and less ambiguity. Reading and writing every day makes us think concisely, increases brain plasticity, and sharpens our minds. Do you want an eye-opening experience? Record yourself talking and you'll witness the huge gap between what you think you sound like and how you actually do. Or write what you're thinking about and then read it a few days later: do you recognize yourself right away in those lines? Are they conveying exactly what you intended? These uneasy practices will boost your self-awareness and, over time, teach you to align your inner and actual self, which assuredly will lead to enhancing your communication skills.

> *The more we communicate, the less we suffer.*
>
> Unknown

You should strive to be a better communicator. The fact that you can effortlessly make sounds with your mouth doesn't mean you are a speaker. The fact that you have ears doesn't guarantee you hear what others say. The fact that you have a brain doesn't mean you accurately understand the information you receive and produce.

The best investment you can make, both for yourself and for others, is to learn to communicate precisely and coherently.

WRITE DOWN

a situation where you failed to communicate your needs:

_____
_____
_____
_____
_____
_____
_____

What do you think you should have done differently?

_____

_____

_____

_____

_____

_____

_____

HEARING
TO LISTEN

listen (v)

take notice of and act on what someone says;
respond to advice or a request

• *I told her over and over again, but she wouldn't listen.*

Do you set a purpose for a conversation before you begin one? Do you consider where a conversation can lead and what outcome it can bring? Do you know what outcome you want? It's common for us to start talking without any substantial reason. More often than not, we talk to share some trivialities or fill awkward silences. Our ability to pronounce words and build sentences allows us to communicate, and that's a powerful act. But we approach the exchange of information lightly — everyone talks, it's not rocket science — and for this very reason, the conversations we have are often repetitive and useless.

Imagine if every time we started a conversation we aspired to hear new information, even if it contradicted what we already knew. Imagine if instead of repeating trivial truths, we asked open-ended questions and listened to the responses we received. Not what we think the answers should be but what we received. Without thinking two remarks ahead, without interrupting or disregarding the other person. Then every conversation would be illuminating and every discussion educational. But alas, that's not how we handle them.

> *The most basic of all human needs is the need to understand and be understood. The best way to understand people is to listen to them.*
>
> Ralph Nichols

> *Listening is not merely hearing. Listening is reacting. Listening is being affected by what you hear.*
>
> Michael Shurtleff

If you observe yourself and others, you'll see that we talk to validate our beliefs, reaffirm our importance, and share our most-likely-to-be-correct views. We can't bear being accused of being wrong. We don't want to look stupid. So we keep our verbal exchanges nice and safe, not to say primitive. If we share information, it's to reassure ourselves and others that we are knowledgeable and experienced. If we ask questions, it's often done out of politeness or confirmation rather than curiosity. Rarely do we say, "I was wrong. Thanks for correcting me," or "I had no idea. Thanks for informing me." We're reluctant to admit our ignorance because it hurts our ego, especially if the subject of discussion is not trivial. Worse, the more important the subject is, the less willing we are to accept that we know little to nothing about it. And we are quick to share opinions that are not really our own but products of ubiquitous media.

But sometimes even safe interactions take unexpected turns. *"How are you?"* — *"Awful." "What a jerk!"* — *"I don't agree with you." "Everything will be fine"* — *"You can't know it."* Moments like these, that throw us for a loop and force us to think about how to handle such hiccups, reveal the perfunctory manner of our talks, how much we rely on auto-pilot, and how superficially we listen to each other. Unusual responses demand us to change our line of behavior and become attentive. And we're not used to being attentive and really listening to each other. Truth be told, it's hard enough to stay alert and manage the thousands of thoughts we have to handle to get through yet another day, so it's no surprise that another person's banal utterances slip through our conscious minds and are treated by our autopilot mode.

> *The biggest communication problem is we do not listen to understand. We listen to reply.*
> Stephen R. Covey

But if we cared to listen, we could have improved our relationships, our understanding of the world, and our place in it. If we cared to listen, we could have learned eye-opening truths that would change our lives. And I'm not talking only about intellectual, epistemic knowledge here, although we would certainly acquire it. I'm talking about a conversational style, a way of thinking, and nonverbal signals that give us valuable insights into human relationships, the world, and ourselves. But we're too lazy and too busy.

I know it's impossible to pay attention to every detail, listen intently to every word, and consciously dissect the meaning behind them. But sometimes we have to make the effort if we want to avoid repeating the same mistakes, offending our loved ones, or misleading others. Sometimes we have to step outside our comfort zone and *really* listen. Because without external *qualitative* information intake, our knowledge deteriorates and our views of the world, relationships, and ourselves get distorted. Without heeding the words and non-verbal clues of others, we become arrogant and narrow-minded. Our egos will be just fine if we stop talking, create silence, and leave it for others to fill. We might learn incredible things that have never before entered our minds. *Will you listen?*

WRITE DOWN

the last time you dismissed someone's words:

_____

_____

_____

Do you think you could have learned something from them if you had listened? If so, what exactly? If not, why not?

_____

_____

_____

_____

_____

THE IMPORTANCE OF YOUR SENSE OF IMPORTANCE

importance (n)

the state or fact of being of great significance or value

• *the importance of honesty.*

A SENSE OF IMPORTANCE

Admit it — you're important. Not just in the way that your words and actions matter, but in the way that you are one of a kind and your significance is undeniable. There's no one else like you. Never was, never will be. You are a king, even if your kingdom is the size of your skull.

If you're quick to deny this truth, then how come you're reading these lines? You'd be long dead if you didn't think your life was worth anything. And you wouldn't be offended if someone cut in front of you in line or talked to you while texting. It's rude of them, but why are you getting disgruntled? What, you deserve to be treated better? *Why?*

We're uncomfortable saying out loud *"I'm a VIP,"* as such behavior is socially condemned, yet we constantly assert this truth through our attitudes and actions. We're quick to label those who cut us off on the road as jerks and those who talk behind our backs as bitches. To put it mildly, we're unsatisfied when we're being ignored or taken for granted. We may not think of ourselves as great people — on the contrary, we're the first to berate ourselves — but deep inside we sense that *"I'm smarter than my neighbor," "I have a richer*

> *The key to success is not thinking you're better than anyone else, but being willing to work harder than everyone else.*
>
> Unknown

> **The biggest challenge in business and in life is to keep your ego in check and stay humble.**
>
> Ryan Holiday

inner world than my colleague," "I'm better than the majority of people."

As with the instinct of self-preservation, this sense of self-importance is vital to our survival. If we want to survive and leave offspring, we must put ourselves first, and take care of our needs as a priority. But this feeling of importance easily turns into entitlement, arrogance, and narcissism. This unconscious sense that we matter most becomes a conscious idea where we think we know better, deserve better, and are better. We wear an invisible crown of exceptionality whose weight distorts our worldviews. We downplay the importance of others and neglect their feelings, knowledge, and aspirations. *I know you're in pain, but my pain is more real; I know you're in a rush, but my time is more valuable; I know you approached the right-of-way first, but I'm in a rush.*

We prefer others to move over and give us the right of way. Such an egocentric approach is inherent to all of us, and so we clash. We violate other people's boundaries and that leads to misunderstandings, disputes, and accidents. We make others and get ourselves upset, angry, and resentful. We're indiffer-

A SENSE OF IMPORTANCE

ent, rude, and condescending. Our sense of self-importance helps us survive individually hurts our social lives. We talk without listening, interrupt without apologizing, and take without giving. These acts are manifestations of our self-imposed superiority. And what grounds do we have for such a presumption? Just a fact that we exist? It's a miracle to be alive, truly (the chance of being born is insanely low — one in 10^2,685,000) and yes, each of us is special and deserves attention. But, at the same time, we are all of the same breed. Asserting one's importance based only on the circumstances of our birth leads to injustice.

> *The problem with thinking you're more important than others is that you stop learning and growing.*
>
> Unknown

In contrast to ill-founded pretentiousness, where we believe we deserve better just because we exist, merit-based significance is earned through doing good for others. People who find solutions to problems and maintain moral principles become authorities naturally. They are respected and listened to. They don't need to get into an argument to prove themselves important. Their productive actions are manifestations of their worth. But merit-based importance is not as widely spread as groundless conceit.

If you'd like to have less hypocrisy and arrogance and more fairness and respect in your life, then the best place to start is with yourself, as always. Dull your thirst for recognition and dominance. Before you put yourself above others, ask yourself this: why do you think that you, your feelings, and your desires are more important? Are there any grounds for your superiority? How does claiming your importance affect your relationships with other people? Does it solve existing problems or does it create new ones?

Through solidarity and mutual respect can we reach desirable outcomes and cease the frustration that comes with social interaction. Assert your grounds in a grounded way.

WRITE DOWN

the reasons why you believe you matter:

_____

_____

_____

_____

_____

the contributions you have made or would like to make to support your beliefs on why you matter:

_____

_____

_____

_____

_____

A NARRATIVE ABOUT NARRATIVES

narrative (n)

a spoken or written account of connected events; a story

• *a gripping narrative.*

a representation of a particular situation or process in such a way as to reflect or conform to an overarching set of aims or values

• *media's narrative of the protest was biased.*

A NARRATIVE ABOUT NARRATIVES

Do Hollywood's ultramundane movie budgets and actors' paychecks bother you? Have you ever thought about why celebrities are paid so much more than people in common professions? Are they more important than doctors, lawyers, and teachers?

> *Narrative is radical, creating us at the very moment it is being created.*
>
> Toni Morrison

I would argue yes. We can ignore some aches, neglect some knowledge, and settle conflicts without involving lawyers. But we can't, never did, and never will exist without narratives and the entertainment they provide. Storytelling has been a part of human history since the dawn of civilization, providing a form of escape and amusement, as well as a way for our ancestors to understand and process the complexities of life.

We constantly tell stories to ourselves and others. The media and entertainment industries just refined the process. Myths, legends, and fairytales are obvious, but they are not the most common narratives we have. Our memories, dreams, and thoughts are the narratives we create and confront daily. They shape our lives. When we reflect on the past, we tell ourselves a story about what happened and how. When we think in the present, we

> **We are the stories we tell ourselves.**
>
> Shekhar Kapur

explain to ourselves what we do and, at times, why we do that. When we imagine ourselves in the future, we visualize our future selves as either successful and loved or unfortunate and lonely.

We create narratives of all kinds to enrich our existence, give meaning to our actions, and evoke emotional reactions from the experiences we have. These narratives, however, don't always correspond to reality. Our mental abilities don't allow us to notice and remember the exact details of the environment and situations we are in. Our multitudinous prejudices preclude us from an impartial perception of the status quo. That's how we distort the truth — through narration. We trap ourselves in illusions and experience maddening frustration when they prove to be wrong. But we can't stop telling stories. Without them, what is left? Emptiness and boredom. In the absence of a narrative, life is devoid of emotion and interest.

When our narratives no longer excite us or leave room for wonder, we turn to stories created specifically to entertain us. We can always rely on movies, TV shows, songs, books, blogs, video games, sports, and social apps to

A NARRATIVE ABOUT NARRATIVES

bring us the thrill we lack in our lives. To feel connected. To gain new experiences. To be someone else somewhere else. In short, to escape.

There's always someone somewhere creating their narratives and bountifully sharing them with the world. As we run low on excitement, we can rely on them to distract and amuse us in exchange for our attention and money. We gladly accept the deal because otherwise we are left to our own devices. If you've ever sat in silence alone for more than ten minutes, you know what your mind can produce — "Nobody loves me," "I'm a failure," "I'm gonna lose my house because of these crazy mortgage rates!" — the horror stories that are capable of throwing off-balance even the most resilient minds. Hence, turning to other people's stories seems sanity-saving.

But it's not. In addition to distorting reality with our biased narratives, we are now exposed to the corrupted stories of others 24/7. As a result, we have a harder time separating truth from fiction and genuine dreams from those imposed upon us. We are encouraged to pretend to be someone we're not. We lose a sense of self.

Some sources of narratives such as myths, legends, and movies are not that detrimental to our mental condition. Due to their clear fictional nature, we can distance ourselves from them, taking in only what we're after, entertainment that is. But can we do the same with present-day CNN news and Instagram profiles? There are times when I fall into their traps. How

> *We live in a world of narratives, and whoever controls the narrative controls the world.*
>
> Caitlin Johnstone

about you? Are you accurate in pinpointing what is real from what is fake?

The act of storytelling invokes imagination and empathy, brightens up days, and alleviates anxiety. When we recall our childhood, share our experiences, read books and watch movies, we gain a better sense of our lives and get our feet on the ground. Unless we are careful, however, the narratives we create and consume can cripple us and cause us to lose sight of what is real. To avoid falling into this trap, we have to remind ourselves that there is no clear-cut truth in what we see, perceive, and think. Neither is there complete honesty in what others choose to say, show, and do. When we encounter narratives that are too positive or too negative, too exciting or too depressing, we should take them with a grain of salt — usually, extremes indicate a falsehood.

Be careful not to follow narratives blindly. Keep a healthy skepticism about your own stories as well as about those of others. And be aware: what we can verbalize and visualize is just the tip of the iceberg of our human psyche. Who knows what lies behind the scenes of our consciousness?

A NARRATIVE ABOUT NARRATIVES

WRITE DOWN

A story of what happened to you yesterday or last week from the 3rd point of view.

i.e. After a long day at work, she decided to unwind by going for a walk in the park.

_____

_____

_____

_____

_____

_____

_____

_____

_____

Write three different descriptions about who you are.

i.e. My name is Alex, and I reside in Springfield with my wife, two kids, and our dog. I earn my living as an electrician, and on weekends, I unwind by watching baseball games with my friends.

My name is Alex and I'm a drone racer. It all started when I bought a drone on a whim and found myself hooked on the thrill of flying. Soon enough, I joined a local club where I met like-minded people who share my interest in the sport and more. Now, I have an escape from the daily grind, and my kids think I'm cool.

My name is Alex, and I'm a troubled sleeper. I'm trying to be an exemplary father, husband, son, and brother, but I feel the weight of all these roles crushing me, especially when I'm alone with my thoughts. I often lie awake at night for hours, tormented by thoughts of letting down my loved ones and the many incomplete tasks on my to-do list.

_____

_____

_____

_____

_____

A NARRATIVE ABOUT NARRATIVES

MAKING A CHOICE ABOUT MAKING A CHOICE

choice (n)

a range of possibilities from which one or more may be chosen.

- *in life, we are faced with a wide range of unfavorable choices.*

MAKING A CHOICE ABOUT MAKING A CHOICE

I once had an idea to write a story with a protagonist who couldn't make any decisions for a single day. But I quickly realized it'd be a short story. A little too short. The story would start and end with only one line: "A man woke up." There's no further development of the plot. The protagonist faces an avalanche of choices as soon as he wakes up: whether to get up or lie down for ten more minutes, what to have for breakfast, check his phone now or later, and many other decisions that, even if left out of the picture, would still be implied. And even if he had stayed in bed all day, that would still be a choice.

We can't have stories without action, just like we can't live without making choices. Our daily lives are filled with thousands of decisions. We don't notice them because the majority of them are automatic. What to eat for breakfast, how to get to work, what to do during a lunch break, where to buy groceries, whether or not to go to the gym, and so on — we've already made those decisions thousands of times and know what to expect. The process of living through mundanity became automatic, saving us frustrations and mental energy.

> *When you have to make a choice and don't make it, that is in itself a choice.*
>
> William James

But once we face a choice we've never made before, or familiar choices in unfamiliar settings, we're caught off guard and need to deliberate. Now we require time and focus to weigh the pros and cons of possibilities, imagine potential outcomes, and select what seems like the most satisfactory option. In the end, this is the reason behind any choice — to avoid misery and achieve well-being. And that's not easy.

Our lives are punctuated by small and big decisions. Some of them, like consumer choices, affect our wallets.* Others, like personal choices, affect our families. The higher the stakes are, the heavier the burden of responsibility gets, and at times, it crushes us — we become unable to make a decision. We procrastinate and postpone making up our minds, or we mull options over and over to arrive at no destination. We can spend months, if not years, choosing what major to study, what job to have, who to marry, and where to live to the point that we get exhausted and choose to let things take their own course. In the end, no matter what path we take, whether it's a path of least resistance or a path of deliberate effort, we'll either regret or be satisfied with our resolutions. These attitudes shape how we feel in life — happy, miserable, bracing, or discouraging.

For more information about consumer choices and how to deal with the paralysis they often bring, check out Barry Schwartz's book The Paradox of Choice.

That's why it's crucial to learn and master the decision-making process. If you stay true to your intrinsic values, there'll be fewer wrong turns and less wasted time. Ask yourself what

MAKING A CHOICE ABOUT MAKING A CHOICE

matters to you most. What are you trying to achieve? How do you plan on getting there? In other words, determine your priorities, goals, and direction. Make your needs clear to yourself. So clear that they're always at the forefront of your mind and you can state them in one sentence.

> *It's not hard to make decisions when you know what your values are.*
>
> Roy Disney

For example, you work on a project that you need to finish before the end of the day. Having worked for a few hours, you decide you need another cup of coffee (or maybe your thing is a walk outside or burpees to get your back on mental track.) Suddenly, you find yourself checking your phone and ten minutes later you haven't achieved anything except getting more frustrated with the world (if you were checking the news) or with your life (if you were checking social media.) Your work progress got derailed. Now it's time to remind yourself of your priority and make appropriate decisions — put your phone away, get your regular coffee, and return to work.

Or let's consider a global picture of your life. You want a loving relationship with your partner, and you know how important it's to spend quality time together. So you want to

> **Life is a matter of choices, and every choice you make makes you.**
>
> John C. Maxwell

plan a date. But then you find yourself shopping online for a thing you don't even really need. An hour later, you're tired and put off your romantic plans. If you find yourself wasting a lot of time and energy on trivial things, write or draw down your priority for tonight/this week/this month and place it right before your eyes. Focus on what matters first. Lesser decisions can wait or be delegated to an automatic process.

Another strategy to achieve optimal decision-making is to consider fewer variables. Nothing is of equal importance. When you try to chase everything, you waste a lot of time and still can be frustrated — a quest for the ideal often ends in failure.

Say you're looking for a sports t-shirt. You go online and see hundreds of them, ready to be purchased with one click. As you read their features, you realize you can't be satisfied with just any old shirt. Now you need a shirt that protects you from UV rays, sweat, wind, mosquitoes, etc. And it should be able to release heat, wick moisture, and dry fast. And you haven't even considered the color and collar yet. Now you're lost in a rabbit hole of a myriad of options looking for that

MAKING A CHOICE ABOUT MAKING A CHOICE

perfect t-shirt. When you think you've finally found one, surprise, it isn't available in your size, and so you continue looking. And looking. And looking. At this point you should be able to see the value of the following suggestion: leave the strained idea of perfection and pursue the valid concept of efficiency. Find an item that fulfills one or two main variables and go about your day. No need to sweat over a sweatshirt, a t-shirt, or any type of shirt. (Did you know there are at least 46 types of shirts? Crazy.)

> *Our lives are a sum total of the choices we have made.*
> Wayne Dyer

Even if you optimize your decision-making process, there's no guarantee you'll always make the right choices. Because you can't predict the future, you can never be sure. But you can't be wrong if you go with this timeless principle: make decisions based on the critical pillars of your character. If you know you hate working with a laptop, for example, then don't do the work that requires you to sit in front of a screen all day. For whatever greater good you may imagine, this choice will still lead to misery. If you know trust is fundamental to your relationship, yet you stay with your partner when he or she violates it, you only prolong the suffering for both of you. No happily-ever-after with one person doesn't mean no happily-ever-after at all.

Life is a springboard for attempts. You try and you fail. You try and you succeed. It's an inevitable cycle. Don't be afraid to take the lead and face the challenges that come with decision-making. The choice is, after all, an opportunity to improve your life. You can either continue living in the same vein, which is also a choice, or you thrive to be better, take risks, and become a better decision-maker. Trust yourself and take the lead.

PS. I intentionally left out the philosophical skepticism regarding free will and the illusion of choice. While they may be valid, they don't contribute to improving your quality of life.

MAKING A CHOICE ABOUT MAKING A CHOICE

WRITE DOWN

a recent medium or large-sized purchase you made. How long did it take for you to decide which option to choose? Are you satisfied with the way you approached the buying decision?

_____
_____
_____
_____
_____

a few principles you will use as guidance the next time you need to make a choice (such as buying a new phone, ordering a dish at a restaurant, or looking for a date.) Arrange them from the most important factors to the least important:

_____

_____

_____

_____

_____

_____

_____

MAKING A CHOICE ABOUT MAKING A CHOICE

Are there any past choices that you regret now?

_____

_____

_____

_____

_____

CARING ABOUT CARE

care (n)

serious attention or consideration applied to doing something correctly or to avoid damage or risk

- *he planned his departure with great care.*

CARING ABOUT CARE

Missed deadlines, poorly executed projects, and forgotten promises — these are the clear indications of a lack of care. You can say you didn't want to, you didn't mean to, you accidentally forgot, and all the other excuses we use to justify our omissions. But the truth is unapologetic — you didn't care or you wouldn't need to come up with excuses in the first place.

> *You can't fake caring. You can't put passion where it doesn't exist.*
>
> Barbara De Angelis

Negligence happens all the time, not necessarily because we are lazy but because we have a limited scope of interests and a finite amount of attention. If we don't find a person interesting, it's exhausting for us to listen to what he or she says. If we don't find a task meaningful, it's arduous for us to do it. If we don't find our lives worthwhile, it's unviable to properly care about anything else. But how do we choose what is worthy?

We can't care about what we regard as dull, useless, and inconsequential and we prioritize what affects our well-being and/or brings positive emotion. Will I be wrong if I say you don't really care about what your colleague ate for breakfast? Or which lacrosse team in a city across the globe reached the quarterfinals? Unless these events have a direct impact

> *The simple act of caring is heroic.*
> — Edward Albert

on you or fascinate you, why should you care? You shouldn't, simple as that. But how about Burundian children, the Benishangul-Gumuz conflict, or the Bornean orangutans' extinction? Do these names ring a bell and a sense of concern? Most likely not. You've never heard of them and they don't affect your daily life. Yet it's harder to admit we don't care about African children, faraway wars, or endangered species, although it's only natural to not pay attention to everything. Do you know anyone who knows about all the injustices in the world and does something about them? I don't think so; we all have limited resources.

But what about cases that elicit regret? What about times when we know we should give attention and yet we fail to do so? We know our parents have been waiting for our call for days, if not weeks, and yet we keep postponing calling them. We know we should have a long-promised lunch with our friend and yet we keep rescheduling it. We know we should perform at work or we lose a chance to get promoted and yet we work half-heartedly. Our friends, parents, and employer can accuse us of apathy and they'd be right. We sabotage our work and relationships, and the truth behind it is ugly: we don't care. Or we don't care enough to act.

Care is evident. It doesn't tolerate pretense. We either help our neighbors or we don't. We either vote in elections or we don't. We either hold on to our jobs or we don't — with all the ensuing consequences. A sense of duty only gets us so far. And then we reproach ourselves of carelessness, regret our omissions, and promise that our future selves will be more attentive. But our actions speak louder than words and we keep making the same mistakes. Unless we get our priorities straight, we'll keep incriminating ourselves over and over again.

How can we recognize when our lack of care has negative consequences and we should do something about it? Take a look at the events in your life that weigh you down. Does your boss keep telling you off for making mistakes? Do you have fewer and fewer hangouts with friends? Does it make you sad that you miss your kids' school events so often? If mistakes are repeated, if friends contact you less and less, if your kids become resentful, it's time to reassess your commitments. Why do you care less about your job, your friends, or your kids? Be honest with yourself, because no one else is listening. Find out what prevents you from putting forth effort. It's most likely not because you're a bad person, a bad friend, or a bad parent as we quickly jump to reproach ourselves and others. Maybe it's because you take on too much? Because you neglect your basic needs? Or because your interests have shifted?

If you don't investigate why you make these mistakes, you can indeed become a bad employer, a bad friend, or a bad parent. Take your time, look at the areas of your life where there are regrets and see how you let yourself down. Most likely, you let the world set your priorities for you and you've lost sight of what matters to you first and foremost. Sadly, it's all too common.

When you establish your priorities, list reasons why you used to care about those things and see if those reasons are still valid. If they are, remind yourself of them. If not, it's okay, priorities change and now you're better equipped to move on. It's quite possible you discover new reasons to care, take note of them too. And if you can't find any reasons, it's time to make some drastic changes in your life. The lack of care, or worse yet, pretended care, leads to misery. And not only yours but other people in your life.

Go through areas of your life — health, family, friends, work, personal development, recreation, et al. Whenever you reproach yourself for not taking care, this is a sign that you actually care about this or that thing, person, or activity. The guilt you feel is a good starting point for action. Think or write, or visualize how a caring version of yourself would act to improve the status quo and lighten the load of regret. Use your imagination. Dream, feel, and live as though your manifestation of care will change your life (*it will!*). You'll get ideas for concrete actions and can start changing things for the better.

Don't wait for times when you'll experience loss, punishment, or deterioration of your health, family relationships, financial situation, or social connections to begin to take action to avoid undesirable outcomes. If the soil of intentions is watered with actions, care sprouts and not only moves you away from bad things but also inspires you to do better, even under no pressure.

And don't put much pressure on yourself. As discussed above, you can't care about everything. You also can't care about what you're told to care about unless you see a need for it yourself. It's possible to pretend that you care, but that pretense will quickly be dispelled and lead to deep disappointments. Instead of being hypocritical, be honest with yourself about what matters to you and what doesn't, and see if your conscience is okay with such distribution or not.

Care is the power that does good and makes the world a better place, and if we take care of this power, it can do wonders.

> *Care and diligence bring luck.*
>
> Thomas Fuller

WRITE DOWN

seven things you genuinely care about:

_____

_____

_____

_____

_____

_____

_____

your actions that demonstrate your commitment to those things:

_____

_____

_____

_____

_____

_____

_____

RESOLVING CONTRADICTIONS

contradiction (n)

a combination of statements, ideas, or features which are opposed to one another

- *not every paradox is a contradiction.*

RESOLVING CONTRADICTIONS

In a word, what is the source of our dissatisfaction, dumps, and poor mental health? Contradictions. We're constantly fighting self-inflicted conflicts that lead to nothing but perpetual unhappiness and emotional exhaustion. Because of the contradictions in our thinking, we grapple with indecisiveness. Even when we make up our minds, expected satisfaction doesn't come. We affirm we know what we want, but we act in defiance of our desires in practice.

> *The test of a first-rate intelligence is the ability to hold two opposed ideas in mind at the same time and still retain the ability to function.*
>
> F. Scott Fitzgerald

We say to ourselves, "I'm tired of my 9-5 office job." Yet, we get up every morning, Monday through Friday, and go to that damnable office we keep complaining about. Do we contradict ourselves? From an outside perspective, it's an obvious yes: our actions don't match our words. But in fact, our actions align with our objectives — we do what we believe should make us happy. In the case of an office job, we choose a stable financial income versus an uncertain tomorrow that comes with unemployment or entrepreneurship. There's no contradiction. There's an unspoken prioritization.

Our brain is well-adapted to categorizing information so that we set priorities quickly

> *The contradictions of life are not accidental. They arise from the necessity of man's double nature and are a sign of his greatness.*
>
> Leon Trotsky

to avoid discomfort. As long as the priorities follow a distinct hierarchy, this process runs smoothly. But once we want mutually exclusive outcomes, which happens more often than we like to admit, we experience inner conflicts. We are unhappy with ourselves. Our self-esteem plummets causing a lack of self-confidence. We self-sabotage. We want to be slim but we eat fast food. We want to learn a foreign language but we don't practice it. We want to be entrepreneurs but we don't take risks.

We are dishonest with ourselves about our true longings. This is the root cause of our inconsistencies and subsequent discomfort. We say one thing but our actions show another. We are either unaware of our actual desires or choose the path of least resistance. In any case, we can prevent clashes if we uncover our true motives. Introspection can resolve contradictions that result from a lack of awareness and self-knowledge.

Pose a chain of "why" questions until you learn the true reasons behind your choices. Those reasons may be ugly, and you may learn that you're lazy, corrupt, or resentful, but for a more harmonious life, ugly truths are better than obscure lies. In contrast to deception, truth allows you to learn and improve. Keep asking why you choose one option over the other until there's no ambiguity. Until you remove all the loopholes in which you should hide your true self. Set your priorities clearly. Embrace reality.

You either want to lose weight and refuse a helping of dessert or you want to satisfy your taste buds and accept the treat. You either want to have your own business and invest your money and time or you don't want to take risks and continue working for someone else. These choices are not about what others think is better or worse. What society thinks is "better" might not necessarily be what your version of "better" is. Their values may not match yours. Only your judgments matter here. To resolve contradictions, you need to set and follow *your* priorities. The better you're aware of the gaps, the fewer inner conflicts you'll experience in your day-to-day life.

Still, a discrepancy is inevitable. We are complex beings. Without the multitude of our feelings, desires, and needs, we would be robots. Besides, contradictions make up creativity. But be aware: they also impede its expression.

I want to conclude by saying that this pernicious tendency to deceive ourselves is natural to all of us. We avoid confronting our real motives because we can get disappointed in ourselves. But without honesty, we'll keep experiencing unproductive disagreements. We'll keep leading discontented lives.

Getting rid of the contradictions that affect us negatively — most of them do — is the key to better mental well-being.

> *Contradiction is the privilege of the living, only the dead have a right to be consistent.*
>
> — Johann Wolfgang von Goethe

When our thoughts, words, and actions are coherent, we create a life in which we are content and productive.

Keep an eye on what thoughts are behind your actions. Devote some time to self-inquiry, and remember that it's only you who can decide what you want and why. *Honestas ante honores.*[1]

WRITE DOWN

a few inner conflicts you have.

_____

_____

_____

_____

_____

Are there any contradictions? Can you identify them?

_____

_____

_____

_____

_____

_____

_____

DESERVING YOUR VALUE

deserve (v)

do something or have or show qualities worthy of (a reaction which rewards or punishes as appropriate)

• *after all the hard work, I think I deserve a break.*

DESERVING YOUR VALUE

You *deserve it.*" Depending on the delivery and context, it can be a reproach or praise. And depending on which one it is, our moods and actions change dramatically. If it's a reproach, we'll feel down, ashamed, and self-pity. We may want to prove such a statement wrong, even if we agree with a reprimand. If it's praise, we'll feel pleased and won't dispute the credit. We'll smile, nod, and accept the positive feedback without subjecting it to an analysis. We're selective like this.

But in both cases, the question arises: who is the judge? Who decides what we deserve and what we don't deserve? What is the basis for such valuations?

We're quick to accept as true what we like and dismiss what we dislike. This tendency is dangerous as it leads to all sorts of biases, false conclusions, and unfairness. And when it comes to giving or taking credit, such proclivity distorts our understanding of the social hierarchy and our evaluation of our own actions, both merits, and misses.

How do you know you did something right and earned what you *deserve*? Was it because it aligned with your moral code or because you were praised for it? Would you do the same

> **"** Your value doesn't decrease based on someone's inability to see your worth. **"**
>
> Unknown

> *A man cannot be comfortable without his own approval.*
>
> Mark Twain

thing you believe is right even if you were later condemned for it? In other words, what matters more: the approval of others or your own approval? What holds more weight?

Abstract reasoning is not always useful since it's not our strongest suit, so let's look at the following scenario.

It's another tedious meeting at work. Your colleague gives a presentation where she makes a critical mistake. No one present, except for you, notices her omission. If everything is left as it is, unfavorable decisions for the company will be made. If you point out the error, the colleague may lose her promotion or even her job. You decide to correct the error because it's the right thing to do. But no matter how tactfully you do it, the colleague loses face, and others present frowned at you — they could well be at her place and you could harm them, too. And only the bosses, if they are present, support you. But their approval is a small thing compared to the toxic attitude you will now get at your workplace for weeks to come.

Did spotting the error make you proud? Most likely, you'd have mixed feelings. But if you didn't point out the mistake, you wouldn't be better off emotionally either, since guilt would creep in. Did your colleague deserve to lose her promotion or job over her mistake? That may be the case, but aren't you guilty of that, too? Also, if you knew others would reproach you severely for doing the right thing, would you still do it? And if the tables were turned and you were that unfortunate colleague, would you support the correction?

My apologies for bombarding you with questions, but how else can you learn more about yourself? :)

Let's look at another scenario. After your colleague is fired (any colleague but if you'd like to make the situation more dramatic, it can be *the* colleague), you're assigned to take care of her unfinished business and use it to prepare a presentation for quarterly reports. Among your colleague's files, you find a presentation that is so well done that it's ready for your management to see, with no extra work required. They love it. They praise you for such competent and quick work and even hint that your promotion is just around the corner. Now, what will you do: correct your bosses' misconception and say that you didn't prepare the presentation and thus, delay your promotion, or take credit for your colleague who is not here to expose your lie?

Who do you choose to be — an unscrupulous colleague who gets promoted or a righteous one who waits longer for a higher position and a fatter paycheck, if any?

There are no clear-cut answers to the above-mentioned questions but analyzing hypothetical scenarios can provide insight into who you are, what you stand for, and what you value most.

BE YOUR OWN GURU

> *A person's worth in this world is estimated according to the value they put on themselves.*
>
> Jean De La Bruyère

When evaluating yourself and others, it's crucial to know what drives your judgments regarding "merit." Because if you don't have a clear understanding of the notion of "deserve," you become a hypocrite. We all do. Unfairness and ambiguity in the world can make us resentful, defeatist, and pathetic.

But when we know what we are, when we own our achievements and mistakes, when we embrace the fact that we don't always know everything and we may be wrong in our judgments of others, we become less conflicted and better members of our family and society.

Giving out rewards and punishments is tough because it calls for ethical decision-making. When you find yourself in challenging either-or situations where you choose between self-integrity or social acceptance, honesty or money, your best bet is to follow your moral compass. If it's not there or neglected, bring it to light and fix the arrows. Write down your principles, define what kind of person you are, and stay true to yourself. There's no quick fix to developing a strong character and handling life gracefully, but knowing what *you value* and defining *your value* sure makes it easier.

WRITE DOWN

things you believe you deserve:

_____
_____
_____
_____
_____

why you believe you deserve those things:

_____
_____
_____
_____
_____

INNER MONOLOGUES

inner (adj)

(of thoughts or feelings) private and not expressed or discernible.

- *inner feelings.*
- *a speaker's inner thoughts.*

monologue (n)

a long speech by one actor in a play or film, or as part of a theatrical or broadcast programme.

- *he had a long and exacting monologue at the end of the film.*

a long speech by one person during a conversation

- *her monologue dominated the entire conversation.*

INNER MONOLOGUES

When was the last time you delivered a monologue to yourself? I'm not talking about abrupt phrases that pop into your head and then disappear just as quickly, but rather a coherent chain of thoughts that leads to a meaningful, digestible conclusion.

Most of our thoughts are random bits that rarely make it to a full-fledged paragraph. They are trite replicas rather than fresh remarkable formulations. Our train of thought travels along the same tracks, without changing speed or destination. We think the same things in the same manner with predictable outcomes.

"*Should I eat a salad for lunch?* (a thought). Meh... (an emotion — not feeling like it). *Next time. Now I need a burrito* (getting a usual meal followed by a worsened physiological state)."

"*Learn how to pass a four-way stop* (a thought), *you idiot*! (an emotional judgment, a heated delivery.) *I'm so sick of these people* (a worn down conclusion, followed by a worsened mind state.)"

"*I'm pathetic!*" (a thought, an emotion, a worsened well-being.)

That's how the mind erodes, that's how it weakens. What's worse, we are unaware of

> " The most important conversations you'll ever have are the ones you'll have with yourself. "
>
> David Goggins

> *Conversations with yourself are the foundation of your inner life.*
>
> Bridgette Mongeon

this calamity or don't acknowledge the significance of such repeated thought action. The wrecking movement continues and we enjoy the ride. These are the usual easy-going thoughts, tinged with rote emotions that yield familiar results.

We might open a window for a short time to get a dose of fresh air — we dare to ask an uncomfortable question or imagine an unsettling scenario. But the fresh air intoxicates, makes us dizzy, and the route we are on gets blurry. Why would we risk our comfort for uncertainty? Such behavior is anti-survival.

You can argue that you're obsessed with innovative thoughts and ideas. You're always ready to leave your comfort zone and always open to the new and unexplored. All very laudable traits, no doubt, but can you specify what new and innovative thoughts you had lately? How do new thoughts come to you? How do you galvanize your energy to produce an unknown in your mind? How do you put a new train car on a new track leading to who knows where? And how come you're not afraid to be a blind driver conducting the explosive mixtures? Because radical ideas, sobering realizations, and embarrassing revelations are explosive — they can change your sense of identity. That is the perilous path not many people dare to follow.

Thinking is tricky and can lead you down the wrong track. But by playing it safe, by having similar thoughts and arriving at similar destinations, by avoiding the risk new knowledge can bring and new landscapes it opens up, you avoid life. You settle for a mediocre existence with an illusionary sense of certainty. You willingly cut short your thorough thought processes and opt for easy superficial answers. Yes, your head hurts less and your day seems more solid and bearable but you rob yourself of a new dimension of your life. A life where you have fewer insecurities and more resilience, where you can grow and succeed on a path of your choosing, less susceptible to manipulation, and more confident in your moral compass. Where you know more and know better.

There's perhaps nothing more peculiar than the human ability to think. If you care about your thoughts, their validity, and their ingenuity, you're ahead of most people who despite having the same treasure, neglect it.

Speak to yourself. Listen to yourself. Mind the quality of your thoughts. Conduct a coherent inner monologue. Do not run off at the first turnpike and don't be afraid of sharp turns. With practice, it'll get easier for you to launch new train cars with original thoughts that lead to new lands. And that's where the fun of being a person begins.

WRITE DOWN

whatever is on your mind right now. Don't stop until you run out of space on the page:

_____
_____
_____
_____
_____
_____
_____
_____
_____

INNER MONOLOGUES

_____

_____
_____
_____
_____
_____
_____
_____
_____
_____
_____
_____

Revisit this page in a few days and reflect on what bothered you and how you expressed your thoughts. See if you can understand your past self clearly.

LIVING IN THE PRESENT

present (n)

the period of time now occurring

- *they are happy and at peace, refusing to think beyond the present.*

What is *now*? And where can we find it?

Oftentimes, we escape "now" by thinking about the past and making plans for the future. *That trip to Mexico was amazing! What should I do this weekend? I should've booked three tickets instead of one. I'll stop at the bank first before going grocery shopping.*

We recall regrets, map out days, dwell on misunderstandings, and plan vacations. These excursions to the past and the future serve a utilitarian purpose — they help us optimize our present. When we're nostalgic or daydreaming without any apparent reason, we optimize our living too. Our memories are concentrated recalls of events that remind us of who we are and what we've been through for better or worse. Our dreams allow us to explore our existence beyond the constraints of our reality; sometimes a few steps, sometimes miles away.

Whether our chaotic thinking leans toward the past or the future, it gives meaning to the present. Our past and future *become* our present. But imagination has its limits, and memory distorts the truth. They create a plausible illusion of life — brighten up a sad past and

> **"** The present moment is the only moment available to us and it is the door to all moments. **"**
>
> Thich Nhat Hanh

> **The art of life is to live in the present moment.**
>
> Emmet Fox

create an exciting future. But, paradoxically, their intervention makes our present less of itself. It makes it what it was or what it could be, but not what it *is*.

And what is it? A boring sequence of repetitive actions. Making a cup of coffee for the nth time, searching for a key that mysteriously disappeared, listening to your friend's broken record, and lots and lots of waiting. Waiting in traffic, waiting in lines, waiting for a microwave to be done. Waiting for things we want or dread, waiting for something to finally happen. This state eats away at our lives and drains our energy. No wonder we try to escape to the past or the future, with the present being so tedious.

But even when things are exciting in the present, rarely do we stay there for long before we look at it through the lens of memories or fill it with plans for "what's next." Our brains jump all over time and space, leaving us with a blurry picture of our daily existence.

While sometimes it's fruitful to limit our perception of the present and run on autopilot instead — after all, life isn't all about being fully concentrated when putting on a sock or scrubbing a toilet and we can brighten these dull tasks by planning vacations or composing limericks — we still get lost in our thoughts too often, letting the present slip right through our minds. And then we wonder how come we fail to notice a key in a prominent place, hear an anxious tone in a loved one's voice, or appreciate the beauty of lush nature.

We long for the early days of our loving relationships when romance filled our hearts, but we do nothing to preserve or rekindle that feeling of love, tenderness, and excitement. We dream of a successful future where we're financially well off but we continue to put off complex and tedious tasks. We accumulate regrets when we could prevent creating them by being more attentive and careful in the present.

"Now" — the most powerful of times — is often overlooked. We live in anticipation of changes but we fail to recognize them when they actually happen. These small tweaks pale in comparison with the far-reaching past events. Graduation day, the first day at work, the wedding day — all were made possible by small steps that didn't look glorious or significant at the time. Yet, they occurred in the present. Changes always occur only in the present. That's why being present for the present is critical. That's when we shape our lives.

If we turn our attention to ourselves in the moment, we'll see what it's like to be us here and now. We'll feel physical sensations — heartbeats, warmth, sounds of surroundings. We'll pay attention to our thoughts, needs, and emotions. We'll be able to see what decisions we make, and why. Life won't just happen; we'll be creating it.

> **There is only one time that is important — now! It is the most important time because it is the only time when we have any power.**
>
> Leo Tolstoy

We don't have to allocate time, find a space, and take a certain pose to be in the moment. Life unmercifully marches forward when we commute to work, cook dinner, observe passers-by, wait in lines, and watch TV. These actions are the time of our lives. What we think and do in those moments impacts what comes in the next second, the next month, and the next year. And even though we never know what will happen next, we might not be under these stars tomorrow, the present moments are even more precious and should be attended to with greater care.

Make the most of this miracle time we call "now." Savor a meal, listen to a melody, observe the environment. Be attentive to your judgments, emotions, and decisions. At this very moment, they're happening, unique and irreplaceable. Make a place for them in your mind and they'll enrich your existence.

WRITE DOWN

what your present feels like at this very moment (its sight, touch, smell, temperature, thoughts, and feelings):

_____
_____
_____
_____
_____
_____
_____

how your present is different now from the time when you filled out the lines above:

_____

_____

_____

_____

_____

_____

_____

LIVING IN THE PRESENT

FILLING UP EMPTINESS

emptiness (n)

the state of containing nothing
- *the vast emptiness of space.*

the quality of lacking meaning or sincerity; meaninglessness
- *he realizes the emptiness of his statement.*

FILLING UP EMPTINESS

There are times when no amount of entertainment, messages, or events can fill the void each one of us experiences at one point or another. There are times when no distraction can pull us further from ourselves. Infinite scrolling and endless texts only exacerbate our neurotic state. The messages of busyness, improvement, and connection bombarding us every minute from our devices dig a deeper hole of loneliness and apathy within us.

We watch a TV show to temporarily escape the boredom of routine and immerse ourselves in an eventful world. But at the same time, we run away from it, checking our phones and sinking into oblivion while the show is still on.

Where are you now? Reading these lines and trying to make sense of its content, or are you thinking of something unrelated, like what you're going to do next? Or eat next? Or maybe you just find yourself reaching for your phone or opening a new tab, without realizing it?

There comes a moment when the flow of information pauses. An episode is over, a feed has been reviewed twice and you are at the

> " *Emptiness is not a mere absence, but a potent presence.* "
>
> Joko Beck

> *The void represents the infinite possibilities that exist before anything is brought into form.*
>
> Jill Badonsky

"You're all caught up" line. Now what do you do? Escape the emptiness thanks to the auto-play feature of a streaming service or the auto-scroll feature of your conditioned fingers? Or will you dare to stop and face the void?

Emptiness is intimidating. Silence and darkness are fertile grounds for fear and anxiety to grow. Silence reveals your voice, darkness highlights your identity. Your lack of purpose and the futility of your hopes are all the more blatant.

In emptiness, there is no consolation and much less fun. There is you, the unhewn, the unkempt, the uncared for; as you, who is afraid of the darkness and flies into the light like a moth to the flame, are at risk of being burnt out.

What are you going to do? Run further from silence into noise or confront an encompassing feeling of numbness?

How about turning me off? I'm annoying, no doubt about that. It's totally expectable that you'll find me confusing and favor another piece of text or video over this one. But as much as I'm annoying and as much as your

FILLING UP EMPTINESS

favorite writer or blogger is a charmer, don't let us do the heavy lifting and fill your emptiness for you. Why not try, for a change, to do the uncomfortable thing? Turn me off, turn your device off (all of your numerous devices, I should say), and just be alone for an hour or two.

Confronting silence is agonizing. It reveals a void that absorbs any joyful moments of your being. Worst of all, silence, as if denying itself, raises questions that, although left unanswered, emit a lot of noise. Who are you? Why are you doing what you're doing? Where are you heading and what purpose are you serving? It's too much to bear for our overfed, media-engorged minds. We are switching off. Or, rather, we are switching on: the screens, the alluring land of possibilities made of millions of colorful pixels.

But then what? Instead of facing the questions that emptiness raises, we help ourselves with another, and another, and another bountiful serving of distraction. Netflix, Spotify, Instagram, and hundreds of other entertainment providers are there waiting for us. Tirelessly. They are what we treat as an antidote to boredom.

> *Exploring the void is an invitation to venture into the unknown, to face our fears and discover the hidden treasures that lie within.*
>
> Debbie Ford

> *The more you leave out, the more you highlight what you leave in.*
> — Henry Green

Meanwhile, boredom is best treated by accepting it. When we deliberately experience boredom, down to its smallest nuances, to the depths where time ceases to exist and the body loses its form, we're able to break free from its depressing spell.

In this emptiness, if you're focused enough, you'll discover that it's not nothing. Emptiness is never truly empty. Life pulses through it: shimmering lights in your closed eyes, tweaking sensations at your fingertips, urges of your hidden desires surfacing in your psyche, trepidations of your unspoken hopes in your consciousness.

When you listen to yourself, you fill the void. When you don't run away from the emptiness, when you don't fill it with whatever dopamine you put your hands on, it becomes tolerable and sometimes even revelatory.

Achieving inner peace doesn't require sitting in the lotus position and trying not to think while thinking; it doesn't require going on a tedious search for meaning; it's not essential to be in a certain place and to be alone.

Surrender is the key. Accept the truth that the feeling of emptiness will come once in a while. That the sense of futility, meaninglessness, and grief for a life you don't live the way you want will show up unannounced to block out any hope.

But it's important to remember that this feeling is only temporary. Life doesn't tolerate a void, and in a minute, an hour, or a day, you'll find yourself back in the whirlwind of earthly things with a smile on your face — messages from friends, new episodes of a show, delicious meals. You can use these events to alleviate your numbness and enrich your mundanity.

As long as you're honest with yourself, as long as you answer the question, "What am I doing right now and why?" you fill your existence with meaning.

Then, even when you turn on Netflix or check your phone, you don't lose yourself. You know when you avoid life and need outlets for your frustration and you know when to accept life's hardships and when you're ready to grow.

You might find that a bit of emptiness actually makes your life fuller.

And now, why not turn off your devices and think about what you're doing next and why?

WRITE DOWN

your thoughts after spending five minutes sitting alone in silence:

_____

_____

_____

_____

_____

_____

_____

how a silent and distraction-free environment makes you feel:

_____

_____

_____

_____

_____

_____

_____

_____

IMPATIENT ABOUT PATIENCE

patience (n)

the capacity to accept or tolerate delay, problems, or suffering without becoming annoyed or anxious
- *we need patience with those who try our patience.*

IMPATIENT ABOUT PATIENCE

Whenever someone tells me "Be more patient," I immediately counter with emotionally charged arguments: "But what if tomorrow doesn't come?" "What if I'm just wasting my time?" "How can you tell me to be patient if you can't possibly know what the future holds?"

Waiting and suffering instead of acting here and now has always filled me with indignity. That approach struck me as procrastination. Or, worse, I saw it as a foolishly confident way of living. How could we rely on fate or "it will all work out, just wait" when we have no idea what would happen but have a chance to influence it by acting in the present?

I've always thought that. Then one day (getting older certainly played a role) I realized: acting here and now is also overconfident since I don't know whether my activity will do more good than harm. I've also started noticing how premature actions can slow down or reverse progress — rushing at work and making a mistake that costs thousands of dollars and a promotion, pushing my body and having to recover from injuries for weeks, failing tests without adequate preparation and having to retake them; and how simple rush can eat up

> *Patience is the companion of wisdom.*
>
> Saint Augustine

> *Patience is not simply the ability to wait - it's how we behave while we're waiting.*
>
> Joyce Meyer

lots of time — forgetting things and having to come back, knocking over a breakable object and having to clean up, doing the work poorly and having to redo it. I didn't get stoical but I got more critical when thinking about patience and reconsidering the previously so annoying advice "Be patient."

My life so far has unapologetically put me in place and shown me that learning, developing skills, and gaining experience take time. It's unavoidable, and shortcuts can backfire. Trying to learn faster results in less effective learning. Multitasking results in poorer performance. Rushing doesn't speed up processes but rather does the opposite. The obsession I had with optimizing and accelerating routine and work processes didn't take me far. One step forward, two steps back. To see it, I had to get three decades under my belt and accept the fact: some walks have to be walked, diligently and patiently.

If you find yourself agitated, irritable, or restless when your affairs aren't in order, when your ambitions and desires are miles away while your reality lags behind, it may benefit you to examine the value of patience. After all, there's a reason impatience is viewed neg-

IMPATIENT ABOUT PATIENCE

atively in our society, whereas its opposite is revered. Or at least it used to.

It has been the case, and still is in large part, that we condemn and are condemned for impatience, especially when it results in disrespect, neglect, aggression, or anger. Whether directed outward or inward, impatience is rightfully to blame when it comes to careless mistakes — in a hurry, it's easy to overlook things and lose awareness and connection with the present — which results in not only time lost but lower self-esteem. We don't achieve what we want when we want it. Even worse, we cause all sorts of harm and have to bear responsibility, from minor inconveniences (a cut finger) to major accidents (a car crash).

Now, however, in our fast-paced age of multitasking and the rat race, impatience has taken on a different connotation — it came to signify success while patience became associated with failure. In the 21st century, it seems odd, not to say inappropriate, to sit in silence by the fireplace or take hour-long promenades in the environs. Such idleness is frowned upon. We're encouraged to be constantly engaged in something, whether it's chatting on social media or working on a commercial project. Or if we happen to sit in place for an hour, we better be meditating. Otherwise, we're quickly judged as lazy by others and by ourselves. But we forget that hurry doesn't make us winners, it just creates the illusion of busyness and importance, blocking our view of the bigger picture. What makes us succeed, though, is perseverance and long-term vi-

> **Patience is the art of hoping.**
>
> Luc de Clapiers

sion, but they require a tremendous amount of patience that most of us lack.

Sometimes we do achieve the desired results by acting immediately. Sometimes waiting pays off. And sometimes there's no need to act at all because we can't influence a situation anyway. Life challenges come in all shapes and sizes and there's no one way to deal with them all. But regardless of circumstances, distressing, getting angry, and resentful over delays and the incompatibility of our wishes with reality doesn't help.

They say measure thrice and cut once because it's a safe approach to take action — it leads to quality results and prevents regrets. And to measure thrice, we need patience.

When you find yourself wanting everything to happen right away, when you feel the need for closure, remind yourself of the truthful cliché: "*Life is a journey, not a destination.*" It works for me and I hope that it'll work for you. And, if needed, revise the chapter "*Living in the Present*" to enjoy and appreciate your journey more fully.

WRITE DOWN

three things you are impatient about:

_____

_____

_____

Can you take any actions to make progress towards them sooner? If so, what specific actions can you take? If not, how could you make the most use of your time while waiting?

_____

_____

_____

_____

_____

_____

_____

THE PATH OF PERFECTION

perfection (n)

the action or process of improving something until it is faultless

• *his art was the perfection of his transformations.*

THE PATH OF PERFECTION

We strive for excellence and impeccability. If not in our actions, certainly in our thoughts and wildest dreams. Who doesn't want to achieve greatness in at least one domain of their life? Who doesn't want their work or character to be recognized as superior? As vain as our motives may be, they inspire us to improve the status quo.

Perfection beckons us. But what exactly is perfection? Life experience shows that it doesn't have a clear, objective definition. Perfection perpetually metamorphoses, depending on what we compare it to, what stage of life we're in and what environment we're in. And more often than not, what mood we're in. What looked great yesterday looks off-putting in the light of a new day; what was considered a breakthrough a decade ago pales in comparison to the cutting-edge innovation of today; what seemed to be a mastery achieved only by a few is now becoming attainable by a larger number of people. The standards in beauty, science, and sports are evolving more rapidly than ever, making perfection vividly unattainable. As a matter of fact, it's always been nearly impossible; just now its

> *The pursuit of perfection often impedes improvement.*
>
> George F. Will

> *Perfection is achieved, not when there is nothing more to add, but when there is nothing left to take away.*
>
> Antoine de Saint-Exupéry

elusiveness is highlighted like never before. When you think you've reached the pinnacle of whatever mountain you've been climbing, seconds away from you lies evidence of how wrong you were to think that. Just go online and see how hundreds, if not thousands of people, have surpassed you at peak conquest. And even if you don't compare yourself to others, if you have your own standards with your uniquely defined summit, perfection doesn't become more achievable because you're your own worst critic.

The pursuit of perfection can paralyze. We become fixated on our shortcomings, doubt our decisions, and abandon our ideas. Rather than move forward, we walk around in circles. "*Should I apply for that great job opportunity?*" "*Should I submit a demo to record labels?*" "*Should I ask the person of my dreams out on a date?*" Often, the answer is no with the reason being "*I'm not ready yet, I must improve first and improve greatly.*" Our fear of failure and desire for perfection prevents us from reaching new horizons. We can remain stagnant for too long if we don't let go of the idea of "perfect time," "perfect place," and "perfect us."

If we're being honest here, sometimes the desire for excellence that prevents us from sharing and completing a project isn't so bad. This helps us avoid the sunk-cost fallacy — abandon bad ideas before they take up too much of our time and resources. Additionally, the world doesn't need everything we create. It's already overflowing with physical and mental garbage, and more often than not civilization won't get better if we finish a manuscript or nail that job interview. But — and this is the keyword here, "but" — we need to keep on creating, progressing, and finishing, otherwise our lives are mere shadows.

Having experiences, making discoveries, and challenging ourselves is the meaning of life (if we dare define such a notion). We have thousands of unanswered questions: who we are, why we do what we do, and what's next. The search for answers to these questions is life itself, and it's accomplished through stepping into the unknown and taking risks that are never done in ideal ways under ideal circumstances. We learn about ourselves and the world around us when we create and dare; there is no clear-cut "ideal" in this modus vivendi. And even if there were, who would be in charge of assigning it? Only us.

The quest for perfection should inspire, not inhibit. There's always something to reduce or add. There's always room for improvement. But this doesn't mean that we should try to achieve flawlessness at all times. Learning to be satisfied with good enough and moving on can bring more value and effica-

> *Perfection is not a destination, it's a journey of self-discovery and self-improvement.*
>
> Unknown

cy than chasing excellence. Our time is finite and it can't accommodate an infinite pursuit of perfection.

Let's trust ourselves to distinguish between the optimal and the superfluous so that we can finish what we started, build on it, and advance. A path of self-actualization, filled with trial and error, is much more worthwhile and productive than a path of perfection as it leads to potentially more achievements than a faultless but purely conceptual idea.

WRITE DOWN

five things you believe are perfect:

_____

_____

_____

_____

_____

Consider how they could be improved*:

_____

_____

_____

_____

_____

_____

_____

_____

*It's a tricky question, but if you give it a try, you'll most likely fill in the lines effortlessly.

THE PATH OF PERFECTION

JUDGING PREJUDGEMENTS

prejudgement (n)

preconceived opinion that is not based on reason or actual experience

- *can experience with the objective world save us from subjective prejudgements?*

How many times have you offered someone to try new foods, new activities, or meet new people, only to hear an immediate *no*? Have you yourself turned down the opportunity to try something new without even considering it?

This is prejudgment in action. We're playing psychics, predicting an unsatisfactory outcome but we're terrible at it[1].

We're all guilty of judging prematurely without sufficient knowledge of a subject, without even attempting to collect data on a subject. We do it all the time and can't help it. How else are we supposed to act? Our brains, as powerful as they are, like shortcuts and use them wherever possible, which leads to numerous biases and fallacies. Most of the time when we need to make a decision, we rely on past experiences, both our own and those of others. The opinions and beliefs we have ingrained which are influenced by our own understandings and those of others' orchestrate our actions in the present. But all this data is incomplete and distorted, therefore it has a high probability of misleading us. But we forget about its imperfection and rarely question the validity of our judgments.

> *Prejudice is a burden that confuses the past, threatens the future, and renders the present inaccessible.*
>
> Maya Angelou

Making decisions becomes more challenging when we face uncommon situations or novel choices. While we still have some inkling of what we deal with, courtesy of half-heard conversations, skimmed media, and intuitive feelings, we probably prejudge and arrive at false conclusions. We let blindly inherited stereotypes rule our behavior and restrict our interactions with novelty, turning us into narrow-minded, stubborn, and contemptuous individuals.

We shut down our minds and carry on with our lives within the guidelines we've established for ourselves. There are certainly times when behavior like this is advantageous — we stay away from the high-crime area in town and we don't gamble because the odds are against us. There are times, however, when limiting our action repertoire leads to scarcity in our lives — we don't pick up a book based on its cover or we don't talk to a person based on their skin color. While we save our time and energy and avoid potential disappointments this way, we also miss out on a potentially positive experience that could make us smarter, happier, and more knowledgeable.

Not everything is to our liking, but that doesn't mean we should reject it harshly. We may try Thai food and don't like it, we may regret attending a heavy metal concert, and we may get frustrated after talking to conspiracy theorists, but we learn from these experiences and are better equipped to make choices next time. This is a post-factum judgment: we've tried, we've learned, and now we know better.

But if we keep shutting the unfamiliar out, if we keep creating boxes for people we don't know and things we don't understand, or if we keep being hypocritical enough to believe we know people and understand things, we become dull, arrogant characters that no one wants to interact with. It takes intellectual humility to acknowledge our limitations and see how wrong our judgments can be. But more often than not, we follow the path of least resistance: we fall victim to confirmation bias and risk turning into dogmatic snobs who are unwilling to leave their comfort zone and take risks.

For our lives to be more exciting and have fewer regrets (we regret what we didn't do more than what we did), we need to keep our minds open. Rather than rejecting unfamiliar things too quickly or too often, we need to make an effort (often a deliberate effort) to welcome them in, if only for a short time; i.e. watch or read a piece of fiction in a genre that we think of as "meh," play the sports we believe we're bad at and won't enjoy, or engage with people from different cultural backgrounds.

Life's journey offers us opportunities to explore new lands and grow as individuals, and

> **The greatest discovery of my generation is that a human being can alter his life by altering his attitudes.**
>
> William James

> *It is not our differences that divide us. It is our inability to recognize, accept, and celebrate those differences.*
>
> Audre Lorde

what we must do to make the most of these opportunities is to subdue our stubborn beliefs and dismissive assumptions.

Next time when you're quick to dismiss novelty or belittle unlike, pause and ask yourself why. Does experience or prejudice dictate your decision?

WRITE DOWN

your beliefs that you are certain are true:

_____

_____

_____

_____

List arguments that will counter the validity of one of your beliefs*:

_____

_____

_____

_____

_____

_____

*to strengthen your reasoning and debating skills.

AUTHENTICALLY ABOUT AUTHENTICITY

authenticity (n)

of undisputed origin and not a copy; genuine

- *this was my first authentic green tea.*

AUTHENTICALLY ABOUT AUTHENTICITY

Media outlets, and thus people around us, have been actively promoting a panacea for success and happiness: "Be authentic."

It sounds beautiful: "au-then-tic." *I am authentic.* Who doesn't want to be authentic? Unique? Inimitable? Unfailingly stay true to oneself?

This trumpet call, however, baffles more than helps as it begs questions: what does it mean to be authentic? What do people who advise it mean exactly? What do they want from us? And, more importantly, what do we want from ourselves? Authenticity is an innate feeling; something we should just know. But we don't. And so we end up wondering and doubting, and spinning further into a quagmire of insecurity and fear.

Without this "authenticity" issue being brought to our attention, we would be totally fine, living in the only way we can — that is, authentically. We are largely guided by our unconscious mind that we cannot control or comprehend, but the unique products of which — thoughts, actions, and feelings — shape us. These processes don't and can't belong to anyone but us. They may be influenced by external forces but even then they

> *Authenticity requires a certain measure of vulnerability, transparency, and integrity.*
>
> Janet Louise Stephenson

> *The biggest challenge in life is being yourself... in a world trying to make you like everyone else.*
>
> Unknown

remain distinct corollaries of our existence. Our thoughts and actions can't be unreal or not original. We might dislike them and resist them, but that doesn't make them fake.

Being authentic means behaving according to one's beliefs and preferences. The intricacy is that beliefs, views, opinions, emotions, and moods are not permanent; they can be influenced and changed multiple times throughout even a single day. Hence, the accusation of fakeness.

Let's say your friend watches you at a party and accuses you of pretending: "You're not like that." But the thing is, you can behave in myriad kinds of ways and still be yourself. And your friend, even you, can't know all these possibilities of you. Maybe you felt tired that day and didn't feel like talking to anyone, or maybe you spotted a former colleague and preferred to keep a low profile, or maybe you met a person you wanted to impress and exaggerated your achievements — these factors influenced your behavior, making it deviate from usual. How you perceive changes in your environment, how you respond to them, and how you adjust or succumb is your distinctive style.

AUTHENTICALLY ABOUT AUTHENTICITY

We all have our ways, our inclinations, and our limitations that make us who we are. Though they might be muffled or influenced greatly by other voices and opinions and covered with dust due to environmental factors and circumstances, they're never lost. We can't help but be authentic, which doesn't always equate to the best outcomes. Sometimes who we are, our personality traits, and our assumptions impede our growth and set us back. This is also a part of life: acting (authentically) stupid and making mistakes from time to time.

Instead of racking our brains over a fancy notion of authenticity, it'd be better to honestly answer the following questions: "What do I want?" "Why do I do what I do?" "How do I really feel about that?" and act accordingly. This method is far more effective to get in contact with ourselves and avoid betraying our principles than the spatial, abstract instruction of "be authentic." That's how we raise self-awareness and build a strong character who can withstand external influences and keep being genuine and true to ourselves.

> *Authenticity is the highest form of self-respect.*
>
> Unknown

WRITE DOWN

situations in which you feel insincere:

_____

_____

_____

_____

_____

AUTHENTICALLY ABOUT AUTHENTICITY

Why do you feel insincere in those situations? Is it to avoid embarrassment? Achieve your goals? Keep private thoughts and desires hidden from others?

_____

_____

_____

_____

_____

_____

If not for those reasons, how would you behave?

_____

_____

_____

_____

ACCUSING EXCUSES

excuse (n)

a reason or explanation given to justify a fault or offence

- *whatever the reasons, they cannot be excuses.*

Have you tried guided meditation? If so, you most likely heard affirmations such as "You are not your emotions. You are not your feelings. You are not your thoughts. They don't define you." Then what does? A soul? An essence? These esoteric notions are too abstract to be used as guidelines for identifying a person. Since we are creatures of narratives and constantly use stories to explain ourselves and others, we must operate with evident truths to avoid self-defeating shams.

I like meditation and the wisdom that comes with it, but mechanically repeating the mantra "I'm not my thoughts" can sometimes do more harm than good. By denying the power of our thoughts to shape our experiences, we are unable to effectively address our bad habits and perilous idiosyncrasies. We play innocent and evade the responsibility of the negative impact we have on ourselves and others.

I know it's comforting to repeat soothing affirmations like "I am not my anger. My angry thoughts don't define me." But your anger exists and hurts others, mentally or even physically. When it does, what is your excuse? A mantra you've learned from a meditation session? How does it help you stop the contagion you propagate?

> *Excuses are the tools of the incompetent, used to build monuments of nothingness.*
>
> Steven Grayhm

> **Excuses are the language of the weak.**
>
> Unknown

And let's not be hypocrites. We're willing to negate our adverse states but what about positive ones? Do you disown them as well? Do you deny the happiness you feel, the kindness you exercise, and the dreams you create? Wouldn't you take credit for the support you give and the joyful mood you experience? Don't their favorable outcomes inspire you to extend and carry out good increasingly?

Everything you do originates in your mind. Your actions are manifestations of your thoughts. They designate your choices, behavioral patterns, attitudes, and reactions that create the unique you. They compose your persona. Take them away and how are you different from the other 8 billion humans on this planet?

You might not like some of your thoughts and the actions they trigger, but it's not a reason to dismiss them. If you dislike the data your conduct sends to the world about who you are, acknowledging its destructive nature is the first step to changing it. Don't divorce yourself from your thoughts, imagining they exist in a parallel universe and you, pure and innocent, have nothing to do with them. This tactic molds detrimental self-delusions.

ACCUSING EXCUSES

Meditation teaches us to take the perspective of an observer and become aware of our thoughts. This precious practice assists us to see the bigger picture and see through temporary emotional states. However, just as you can't cure an illness solely by observing it, you can't break free from habits by abstracting your mind from them. The transition happens when a problem is admitted, not denied. Repeating affirmations about a better you is a sound starting point to envision what you're thriving for. But for an actual change to happen, you need to act and be accountable for the consequences your actions bring. Otherwise, you follow the path of least resistance and never achieve your ambitions.

You are your thoughts and emotions. Though they may not define you permanently, they create your actions and choices. When you acknowledge this truth, you access the mighty power of your mind: the ability to change what you want to change.

Take ownership of both the good and the bad you have within you. Recognize your achievements and confront your demons. Only then can you lead a more significant and meaningful life.

> *Excuses are the justification for mediocrity.*
>
> Unknown

WRITE DOWN

beliefs you hold about skills and abilities:

_____
_____
_____
_____
_____
_____
_____
_____

ACCUSING EXCUSES

Are there any beliefs that are actually excuses rather than facts?

_____

_____

_____

_____

_____

What counter-arguments could you provide to the spotted excuses?

_____

_____

_____

_____

_____

DISAPPROVING APPROVAL

approval (n)

the belief that someone or something is good or acceptable

- *in some cultures, approval of opioids is significantly higher than approval of alcohol.*

DISAPPROVING APPROVAL

Many people are stuck in a cycle of posting online and checking what comes afterward — likes, dislikes, and comments. They worry about the engagement rate and sweat over the sacred conversion rate.

We're willingly making ourselves vulnerable by putting our thoughts, ideas, and creative works out into the online world. And then when we don't receive the feedback we expected, we suffer. (Surprise!)

We seek outside validation which, more often than not, threatens our self-acceptance. We make our imperfect lives look perfect. We hide our insecurities and showcase our best selves. We selectively expose our lives thinking that we have control over how others see us. And with all these extra efforts — hours of photo/video shooting, writing, photoshopping, editing, and redoing — we still get a disappointingly low number of likes and generic comments.

We share information with the world and then worry about its response. How many likes have my photos/posts/videos generated? Is it enough, or do I now look like a fool? It gets to the point where we don't accept our-

> *Care about what other people think and you will always be their prisoner.*
>
> Lao Tzu

> *The best way to gain approval is not to need it.*
>
> — Hugh Prather

selves unless we are accepted by others. We allow others to control our self-worth and dictate our failure and success.

In this day and age, we can access the immediate response that reveals our significance easier and faster than ever. With a single click, you start collecting data on how your peers relate to you. Do they like or hate you? Are they on the same page as you? Do they care about your existence?

The more we look at online metrics, the more obsessed we become with them. Our self-love depends on numbers, which are, in truth, misleading. We attach great importance to them, so much so, that we experience a racing heart, dry mouth, upset stomach, and other physical responses that have a detrimental effect on our bodies. *Is your worth in the eyes of others worth it?*

It doesn't end with physical consequences, though. It impedes our creative process and self-expression. We inhibit our urges to innovate so that we avoid risking our social image. It's not always a bad thing. Some constraints are welcomed. The majority of us won't like other humans walking around naked, defecating on streets, and building castles with it.

DISAPPROVING APPROVAL

(Don't ask me how I came up with this example.) But it's not the extreme that worries me. The troubling extreme is that we're becoming slaves of meaningless button clicks and screen touches. Just imagine how you'd feel if you received one hundred likes within one minute. And now imagine what it'd be like to get one hundred dislikes within one minute. There are two of you now. One is elevated and another one is deeply miserable.

What if the validation you so badly wish for doesn't come? Would you interpret it as a failure? Would you identify yourself as a loser? Or would you just eat a bucket of ice cream and hope tomorrow will be a better day?

It takes resilience, confidence, and pride to stay true to our values and beliefs regardless of external evaluation. These qualities of a strong character are forged with years. But at this moment, just understand that you're not the $100 bill that everyone likes. Others are watching you and judging you and vilifying you. You're judging and belittling others, too. When we share online, we should be mentally prepared for rejection and not let it define us.

When participating in the social media world, sign an agreement with yourself. Instead of checking metrics and seeking approval over and over again, use your time for growing and creating. There is a line between pleasing yourself and pleasing others; between creating to fulfill oneself and creating for the sake of others' approval. What style is more appealing to you?

WRITE DOWN

names of people whose opinion of you value:

_____

_____

_____

_____

For each person listed above, estimate how well they know you (you can use a scale of 1-10):

_____

_____

_____

_____

_____

Consider only listening to feedback about yourself, your work, and your choices from those you value, respect, and who know you well. Try to limit reacting to the opinions of everyone else, and use the saved time and energy to better understand yourself and progress towards your goals.

ON MEDIA NOISE

noise (n)

a sound, especially one that is loud
or unpleasant or that causes disturbance

• *please reduce noise, and not just auditory noise.*

ON MEDIA NOISE

A flux of snippets of others' lives, scraps of news, relatable opinions, trivial advice, and endless sales. You are the spectator and the creator of this online shitshow. Are you, as I am, weary of the media noise that we seemingly voluntarily dive into every single day of our existence? Success stories, eye-catching glossiness, whimsical humor... Everyone has a desperate need for recognition. Everything is with the article "the" and the ending "-est". The smartest, the prettiest, the funniest. Mediocrity is dressed up as superiority, ruler of this virtual reality parade.

We scroll through Instagram and I'm introduced to the pinnacle of human beauty. We watch YouTube and are shown life on steroids, exaggerated to the point that it's no longer recognizable. We read Twitter and we're being educated about the all-mighty yet frail culture we're in.

But we accept the rules of the game, participate in it, and, even more so, we're privileged to be a part of it. (After all, being online is reliving many lives instead of one, and usually, those lives are better than the ones we have. They are created to be better than the ones we have.)

> *The quieter you become, the more you can hear.*
>
> Ram Dass

Lamenting about how pervasive the Internet and social media can be is akin to beating yourself up for eating pizza. You could say no, ignore the numerous pizza signs and make a healthier choice; but then where will you look for the joy of your existence? In salads? Or in Montaigne's philosophical tractates? Perhaps if you lived in an alien world where silence and plain food were enough to make you love your life, this could work; but it's not enough, not for the world we live in today.

You and I have already discovered the gamut of rich flavors that pizza can offer. We have been introduced to endless entertainment, and now we don't want to give it up. Consumption itself is not an inherently bad course of action; it serves to sustain life. What makes it harmful is the way we consume — how, when, and in what quantities. Mindless, chaotic gluttony is what hurts.

The Internet and media are not poisonous or noisy by default. The way we interact with them makes them as such. Our short attention spans and mindless devouring reduce everything we consume into nothing more than garbage. We read distractedly, we watch in the background, and we idly listen while only lending half an ear. We unconsciously consume from these sources, unaware of our own pliability. As a result, we're constantly engulfed in an infinite cacophony of noise.

The cacophony of the successful success and famously famous, of elusive happiness and the illusion of reality. Endless dreams, hopes, and promises are given to us without us asking for them.

ON MEDIA NOISE

I'm not a fan of this constant noise. Yet, here I am, contributing to this disturbing song.

Why? It's not like I have any compulsive need to do so or believe that I have something to say that I feel needs to be said. My creativity is easily extinguished by comparison to the artificial perfection consumed daily on my screen.

> *In order to understand the world, one has to turn away from it on occasion.*
>
> Albert Camus

Like you, I am both a spectator and participant in today's media. And like you, I have opinions, beliefs, and thoughts.

Instead of getting lost in the intricacies of my disturbed mind, I decided to pour them out on this digital paper. This should clear up some of the mental clutter that endlessly accumulates.

There is a chance that you, after consuming these lines, will find them to be relatable, questionable, or provoking. There's also the chance that you might create your own meaning that will propel you to improve your present.

After all, you are the one who has the power. It is through your intentions that you have the ability to turn gold into shit, and shit into gold. You can find critical insight into your

> *Silence is the sleep that nourishes wisdom.*
>
> Francis Bacon

own psyche and learn vital information that will make your life more bearable and, maybe, if you're open to it, more fulfilling.

Whatever noise inundates your consciousness, you have an ability — however imperfect — to filter that endless flow of information into something capable of enhancing your own life.

That's the reason I am here — helping you and myself to discover the elusive concept of rationality. Armed with this ever-changing notion of finding meaning, we will dive deeper into an experience of what it is like to be a human in the 21st century.

WRITE DOWN

how much time you spend on your phone each day:

_____

_____

Your phone likely has a feature that shows you this figure. If not, estimate.

When using social media, do you typically use the search bar to find specific content, or do you tend to scroll through your feed?

_____

Write down specific content you could search for on social media instead of mindlessly scrolling:

_____

_____

_____

_____

Challenge yourself to use social media only by searching for specific pieces of information, ignoring what the algorithm suggests for you.

VALUING VALUE

value (n)

the importance or worth of something for someone

- *nothing has any inherent value except the value we put in it.*

VALUING VALUE

Some things in life have a clear value, however arbitrary — i.e., a price tag. Others have no tangible indication of worth, and yet, are way more valuable. So valuable in fact that no price can truly represent them: family, honor, trust, self-actualization, logic, etc.

We often don't realize our values until they've been compromised or taken away from us. Likewise, we don't realize we betray them until our well-being deteriorates. We feel down but don't know why. This "why" is a reflection that we lack what matters most to us. Time spent with family and friends makes us feel better but pushes back meetings with them to deal with the hustle and bustle of life. Our art hobby gives us a unique sense of satisfaction, but we don't practice it as much since there's always something "more important to do." Yet, no matter how many boxes we've checked on our to-do list, and no matter how many so-called important things we've handled, we still feel miserable. We betray what we regard as high worth, and whether or not we realize it, this leaves us feeling empty, inadequate, and sad.

In this book, the word "value" runs like a red thread. It's the basis for all our decisions. Ev-

> *Values are what bring distinction to your life. You don't find them, you choose them.*
>
> John C. Maxwell

ery action we take demonstrates to the world (unfortunately, not always to ourselves) what we believe is important. Our values also form the basis for our goals, which give meaning to life and make it more satisfying. If we lack a clear understanding of our values, we're more likely to overlook the discrepancy between our values and our goals, and consequently, make regrettable decisions. When we don't know what we stand for, what we're committed to, we condemn ourselves to a miserable existence where it feels like the world is against us and where we're not understood, when in reality we're the ones who act against ourselves and don't understand ourselves. How can we solve the problem of misleading ourselves? By defining our values and staying true to them.

Consider what would leave you despondent if taken away from you. Family, health, career, or travel may come to mind. But don't limit yourself only to tangible values; abstract ones such as kindness, justice, verity, and honor are equally important.

Now consider what you are willing to make sacrifices for. Are these the same notions you outlined in the previous step? If so, you're being honest with yourself, which is commendable. If not, they aren't your values, only ideas that make you feel good about yourself and nothing more.

Some of your identified values will turn into sacrifices — things you'll give up for something else you consider more important. Sacrifices are inevitable since our time, attention, energy, and money are limited, which forces us to prioritize. There are times when we need to make choices, such as between career or children, vacation or investment, honesty or fairness, and although these decisions aren't always so dichotomous, trade-offs will be required. One thing will come out better or get more of our attention and care than the other. That's who it is for all of us.

Having a clear sense of your values hierarchy will help you avoid unsettling surprises. Let's say you always wanted to be a great parent, and then one day you found out that your children didn't really like you. How come? Looking at your actions, you might see that you prioritized work, and consequently, you kept missing your kids' baseball games and didn't go to amusement parks with their friends, giving them the responsibility of their friend's parents, and didn't pay much attention to their interests. Maybe you even got angry with them when they interfered with your workflow and raised your voice. Despite your desire to be a great parent, you put work above your children. The mystery is revealed.

It's important to mention here that your value hierarchy may not align with those society deems moral and righteous. If that's the case, you have two options: either find ways to rec-

> *Your values are a reflection of who you are and what you stand for. They define your character and shape your destiny.*
>
> Unknown

oncile with this disparity, or adjust your value system to align it better with those of your environment (which is a more beneficial strategy in the long run). In either case, you need to determine your values and make sure they're ranked. You can write out your values (or find a list of values on the Internet, if you're still unsure what they could be) and assign each a weight (on a 5- or 10-point scale). Don't chase too many, otherwise learning about priorities will become paralyzing. They all should be the ones you cannot imagine your life without.

When assigning points, you can be tempted to arrange them as your environment dictates right. But it's crucial to be honest with yourself. Visualize to understand what makes you feel more satisfied: a meeting where your boss praises you for the results you achieved in the last quarter, and emphasizes in front of your colleagues how well you executed a deal or a baseball game where you see your child running all the bases quickly and scoring winning points for his team and then gets giddy with joy as only kids can.

As you imagine scenarios relating to each value in your list, please don't judge yourself for your preferences; there is no "good" or "bad" judgment if you're honest with yourself. Although it'd be more accurate to say: a bad judgment is one that contains more lies.

When you line up your values in such a schematic manner, all of the secrets become clear. You may experience emotions of shame and disappointment. This is all acceptable — we are on our way, not at the destination, and we can still change our behavior to reduce the dissonance between what we think we value and what we actually value. If you experience negative emotions when looking at your values hierarchy, it's a sign that you either don't accept your values and are hurt by how they contrast with what you should consider important (for instance, your surroundings believe that children should always come first, but you admit you're much more satisfied with your career achievements than being a parent) or now you realize that your actions don't support your values (you know and feel that your children are number one to you, but you work overtime and miss important events in their lives.) In any case, don't degrade yourself. By exposing such painful inconsistencies, you're already starting to move in the right direction.

If you've been honest, you've learned a lot about yourself and now have a better idea of what a "happy life" means to you (hint: one that aligns with your values.) When you're aware of your principles, you can adjust your behavior accordingly, which leads to peace of mind. Let's say you learned that your children matter to you more than any career height but you still want to pursue your professional path. You can set a rule for yourself that for every three times you choose kids over work, you commit one act where work comes first. Of course, this ratio of 3 to 1 is arbitrary and not weighted according to the magnitude of events. But, the main point here is to find a compromise that will make you feel good about your decisions without feeling guilty for missing out on one or another

> *Values are not just nice to have, they are essential to our well-being. They provide a sense of purpose, direction, and fulfillment.*
>
> Arianna Huffington

front. To put it simply, experiment to find a balance that works for you and keep it in mind when saying "yes's" and "no's" in different areas of your life.

Life is not as polarized, and one group of values doesn't always oppose another. But one group of values will always — *always* — receive more of your resources (time, money, and energy) than the others. Hence, it's best to work with up to ten values at a time, otherwise, you may get completely lost and let things drift away.

There is another caveat: one group of values may be represented by conflicting behaviors. Let's say you value your health and decide to follow these three essentials: adequate sleep, regular exercise, and balanced eating. But when you try to implement them into your busy schedule, you see a clash: you can exercise only before work but then you have to get up earlier, which cuts off that precious hour of sleep.

If you spot such conflicts, review the assumptions that created them. Is your day really so full of activities that are more important than your health, leaving you with no time to exercise later in the day? If not, review your agenda and make a slot for sports. If yes, reconsider your evening routine so that you go to bed earlier. Or maybe you'll decide you can't have both sufficient sleep and regular exercise (unlikely, but still), and you'll prioritize one over the other. The order in which you rank your values will help you organize your time most efficiently.

As a final note, I'd like to draw your attention to another kind of value: the value of oneself. You can identify and rank your values and still be dissatisfied with yourself and your life. That happens when you lack self-worth and, consequently, devalue your actions, your accomplishments, your possessions, or even your very life. When you have low self-esteem and downgrade your persona and achievements, you can't be happy. That's just how we are — objective truths mean nothing if our subjective beliefs contradict them.

The basis of self-value is self-respect. Pay attention to how you treat yourself, your time, and your deeds. Do you hold them and yourself in high regard or do you think neither you nor your actions matter? By devaluing yourself and your endeavors, you let your life chance and miss out on opportunities that could enrich your existence. While we are cosmically insignificant, we have an enormous impact on our lives and on those around us, and are accountable for the rewards we reap and the missteps we make. We cannot afford to be so irresponsible as to think we are unimportant and our actions don't matter. This road leads to a dead end — a meaningless life.

How do you feel about your past accomplishments? Can you name them? And what do you consider an accomplishment? If your idea of achievement is only something big, like securing a six-figure salary, and everything that came before — studying at university, passing an exam, graduating, writing a resume, failing your first interview, finding your job, being dismissed, being promoted — isn't all that important, you're negating your merits, which makes you less confident and less persistent. Every experience, every link in the chain of events, brings you new knowledge and broadens your horizons. You're better equipped to make wise decisions in the future if you acknowledge your past and understand what it means to you.

The world is quick to tell us what to value, and its suggestions might be rooted in age-old wisdom. But for us to lead a meaningful life, it's not enough to accept these values on faith. We need to genuinely agree with them and act in harmony with them. As this chapter showed, figuring out our values can be challenging, but if done diligently, it can relieve guilt and prevent regret.

WRITE DOWN

the top three things that matter to you in each of the following areas of your life. Be specific:

physical and mental health

_____

_____

_____

personal relationships and family

_____

_____

_____

career and education

_____

_____

_____

personal development and self-expression

_____

_____

_____

Arrange the noted values in order of importance, from most to least important. Keep the list to a maximum of five items:

_____

_____

_____

_____

_____

It's a tough task, but trimming down to the core essentials can help you make decisions that you won't end up regretting.

Come back to this list whenever you feel overwhelmed or lost due to external demands. It might also come in handy when making New Year's resolutions ;)

SABOTAGING SELF-SABOTAGE

sabotage (v)

deliberately destroy, damage, or obstruct (something), especially for political or military advantage.

- *the basis of their subtle sabotage was double language.*

SABOTAGING SELF-SABOTAGE

We don't believe we can act against our goals until someone else points that out to us: "*Why are you doing this?*" "*You're self-sabotaging.*" And even then, it's unsettling to admit. Who in their right mind would hinder their progress and undermine their success? But if we look closely, we do this quite often. Consciously or not, deliberately or simply out of laziness, we go along with bad habits. We put a spoke in our wheel, ignore our merits, and regard our accomplishments as insignificant in-between aughts.

Many of our problems arise due to self-sabotage, an elusive problem that takes a lot of effort to recognize and resolve. It hides behind many masks, such as a rickety self-esteem (we think we're not good enough), low self-confidence (we think we can't do it), and imposter syndrome (we believe our success to merely be luck, that we are unworthy of what we have attained).

Self-sabotaging acts are obvious if we take a step back and look at our actions from the outside. Do we watch TV instead of following our plan to write a CV? Do we eat a cookie while on a diet? Do we bring up a former offense in a current quarrel? Do we say *yes* when we want to say *no*?

> *The most insidious form of fear is self-sabotage.*
>
> Unknown

> **The mind is everything. What you think, you become.**
>
> Buddha

When our intentions are at odds with our actions, that's a sign we're engaging in self-sabotaging behavior. In some instances, it may even seem virtuous: we conduct thorough research, we work long hours, and we volunteer to take on more tasks. It's only the ostensive consequences of such behavior — procrastination over other tasks, delayed and poor work performances, and burnout — that reveal our failure to achieve our objectives.

Other manifestations of self-defeating behaviors are more concealed and subtle. We don't call a loved one back to apologize for our rudeness. We make mistakes and don't forgive ourselves. We are praised and all we do is lower our eyes and brush off the positive result of our work. As a result of these behavior patterns, we sabotage our values. We want a loving relationship, we want to stay motivated, we want to have peace of mind and yet we act counterproductive to them. We become frustrated and resentful of ourselves. We blame ourselves for not being motivated enough, strong-willed enough, courageous enough. We can even start wondering "*What's wrong with me?*"

Negative self-talk, pessimistic outlook, striving for perfection make us more susceptible

SABOTAGING SELF-SABOTAGE

to repeating the undermining behavior. We can even fall into thinking: "*How can I expect any better from myself, such a [berating name of your choice]?*" This slippery slope often leads to low satisfaction in one's life and self. We no longer aim higher, we no longer try harder. We prefer to play it safe, to the point where our lives become unremarkably dull. And then we blame ourselves, and so the vicious circle continues.

To break free of this destructive cycle, we must recognize where our goals conflict with our actions. Self-sabotage occurs when our fear of threats is stronger than our desire for victory. As a way to see these instances, we can dissect our behavior into its base components: a goal/desire → an act, and look at them purely schematically, factually: *I want to lose weight* → *I eat cookies*; *I want a new job* → *I don't send out my resume*; *I want to resolve an argument I'm having with my partner* → *I keep bringing up old insults.*

As we observe our behavior dispassionately, we can see when we get in our own way, when we act as if we don't believe in ourselves (that we can lose weight, that we can get a new good job, that we can communicate effective-

> " *Self-sabotage is like driving with one foot on the accelerator and the other foot on the brake.* "
>
> Unknown

> *Self-sabotage is the art of getting in your own way.*
>
> Unknown

ly), when we act as if we are unworthy of a good job, a loving relationship, and above-average achievements. Maybe we don't always get right to the root of our beliefs, but at least we expose them for what they really are: pervasive destructive thoughts. There's a solid start to making changes.

Perhaps, after exposing inconsistencies in our thoughts and actions, we'll see that by not taking credit for our achievements, we deprive ourselves of encouraging feelings and motivation boosts, making us learn slower and more vulnerable to our self-critic; that by not apologizing for our rudeness to a loved one and continuing to hold grudges we degrade the quality of our relationship and hurt both parties; that by pushing ourselves and working long hours, we end up making more mistakes and depleting our energy reserves that leads to burnout and setbacks. Perhaps we'll see that dwelling on mistakes we made long ago prevents us from acting, taking risks, and exploring new possibilities. But we all make mistakes, and the best thing we can do is learn from them and move on.

It's quite possible we won't understand all the motives for our self-handicapping behavior but simply acknowledging that self-sabotage exists, spotting its manifestation in our actions, and recognizing its negative impact on our lives will loosen its invisible stranglehold. When we become more aware of our detrimental habits, we're better equipped to deal with them. For instance, the next time we eat a cookie while on a diet, rather than blaming and berating ourselves for our weaknesses, we'll be able to recognize that we're self-sabotaging our weight-loss plans. Then the next beneficial step would be asking ourselves why we do it. Maybe we don't believe we can lose weight. Then we'd be better off dismantling that belief. For that, we can read stories of people who succeeded (hundreds of thousands of them) and change our views on the matter. Or maybe we have conflicting desires — we crave a cookie and a slimmer body? Then we'd be better off refreshing our motivation for losing weight (we can try positive and negative visualization techniques) so that the desire for a slimmer body is stronger than the desire for sweating.

There are conflicting urges and wants in us, and the ones with the strongest grip win. Unfortunately, all too often, noxious desires have greater power than expedient ones, and so we tend to self-sabotage. Defining our goals clearly, recognizing our tendencies to act against them, and taking deliberate steps to rectify our inadequate beliefs and counterproductive actions that follow are essential to reaching our objectives and being at peace with ourselves.

WRITE DOWN

your habits that hinder your progress towards your goals:

_____

_____

_____

_____

_____

_____

_____

SABOTAGING SELF-SABOTAGE

For each habit, suggest an action to minimize its adverse effects. Be specific.

For example,

- Habit: Checking social media dozens of times a day
- Action: Check social media twice a day (during a lunch break and after dinner) for no more than 20 minutes at a time.

Habit: _____

Action: _____

Habit: _____

Action: _____

Habit: _____

Action: _____

Habit: _____

Action: _____

Habit: _____

Action: _____

Do you hold any beliefs about yourself that hinder your progress towards your goals? In the left column, list them as they are, and in the right column, list the opposite of each belief.

For example:

It's too late to pursue my dreams. ———————————————— —>

_____ —>

_____ —>

_____ —>

_____ —>

_____ —>

_____ —>

_____ —>

_____ —>

Now is always the right time to pursue my dreams.
_____

_____

_____

_____

_____

_____

_____

Reread the right column and reflect on evidence in your life or the lives of others that support these beliefs. It may be challenging to let go of long-held beliefs, but being open and curious to new evidence, rather than dismissing it quickly, can lead to positive shifts in your perspective and increase your chances of achieving your goals.

PRIORITIZING PRIORITIZATION

priority (n)

the fact or condition of being regarded or treated as more important than others

• *the safety of the country takes priority over any other matter.*

PRIORITIZING PRIORITIZATION

I don't buy the phrase: "I don't have time for this." What I actually hear is: "This is not my priority."

It's okay to refuse to do things as long as we are honest about what matters to us first and foremost. Everything can't be of equal importance. That's why we need priorities, things that we regard as more important than others. We only have one body and one brain, so we can't help but divide our attention in order to get things done.

But this division should be calibrated, otherwise we risk always bringing up the excuse '*I don't have time*.' Look at your daily life. You always find time for sleep and food (otherwise, you wouldn't be reading these lines.) And you always find time for things you care about and enjoy (otherwise you'd be too depressed to read these lines). Where you struggle is allocating time to activities you dislike — you can postpone unpleasant tasks for days and weeks, or even years.

Your avoidance and omissions, order, and preference are tools for optimizing your life. Every day you choose some activities over others, and your choices either contribute to your goals or hinder them. Think of your past

> *The things that matter most must never be at the mercy of the things that matter least.*
>
> Johann Wolfgang von Goethe

achievements. Why did you accomplish what you did? Coincidence? Luck? I don't think so. All your achievements are your past priorities. You chose to devote your time and energy to the tasks you found important. If you were serious about your goals, you arranged your routine around them and made needed sacrifices, so now you can see the results. Whether we like it or not, the way we spend our time determines the quality of our lives, and not our surroundings, genes, or luck. The time is constant, we are volatile.

We all have 168 hours a week. For most of us, 45% of it is spent to simply keep ourselves functioning (~56 hours goes to sleep, ~10 hours to hygiene, ~10 hours to food preparation and consumption). What we do with the rest shapes our lives. Most of us devote about 25% to work (35% if we factor in commute times and long hours.) The remaining quarter should be "*me time*," the time we rely on to improve and enjoy our life, but instead, it's spent waiting, running errands, and checking the news. And then when we say '*I don't have time*' to our friends, goals, or sports, we may not even feel guilty. We indeed were so busy we didn't even make the time to just be.

For an end to this excuse, learn how you allocate your weekly time budget, that is 168 hours. Create a table and note how many hours you devote to which activity. Put in essentials — sleep, food, hygiene — first, then fill in hours for work, family, and friends, and then for the rest — sports, logistics, learning, and procrastinating. Leave out a few buffer hours. Now see how your predictions follow your reality. If you "lose time" (you spend hours on activities that you didn't allocate time for), modify your table to include recurring time-consuming tasks or eliminate them altogether. The idea here is to create time blocks for what you care about. Even an extra hour a day (extra seven hours a week) can be enough to make significant progress in any endeavor: training for a marathon, writing a book, or learning a new programming language.

Let's say you want to learn a programming language within three months and not a year. Now you have a solid springboard to find the time to accomplish your goal in a timely manner. Revise your table and spot activities to optimize. Trivial tips like grocery shopping once a week, meal prepping, batch cooking, and turning off your devices for a few hours in the evening will make room for your more meaningful pursuits. The freed-up hours, if used wisely, can radically change your life.

To succeed in your pursuits, you don't need magic powers, superior intellect, or exceptional talent. What you need is to learn to prioritize. Focus on the 20% of tasks that drive 80% of results and ignore the rest, that is an endless stream of distractions and temptations.

> *Your priorities aren't what you say they are. They are revealed by how you live.*
>
> Unknown

> **You have to decide what your highest priorities are and have the courage - pleasantly, smilingly, non-apologetically - to say 'no' to other things.**
>
> Stephen Covey

Such an approach to performing is hard. It requires tremendous commitment and sacrifice, which only a few of us can endure. If you're already on the path of austerity and obstinacy, you witness how your determination falters from time to time and how it gets increasingly difficult to stay motivated. We tend to lose sight of the bigger picture and succumb to immediate gratification. And only those of us who can find our way back on track, who preserve long-term vision and have strategies to deal with distractions, achieve success. Would you consider yourself one of them?

The power of prioritization holds true not only in the professional realm but also in the personal sphere. Do you want to be happy in relationships? Always make time for your loved ones, and show them you care about them through your actions. Do you want to be a good parent? Always put your kids first, listen to them, and support them.

But here's a caveat: your priorities from different areas of life — work, family, personal development, health — compete for your time and resources not just within their realm, but across them too. If you want to achieve exceptional results in your main pursuit, you have no choice but to choose it over everything else. Do you want to be the CEO of a company? Put your work first, devote the most time and energy to it, and accept that your personal life will suffer. Painful clashes are inevitable. If you cherish yourself with the idea that you can have it all, then you settle for average results across the board. Which is not necessarily a bad thing. Great achievements demand great sacrifices, and not everyone's up for that. One would argue that a balanced average brings more happiness than extreme exceptionality.

If you have a goal you wish to accomplish, however, not much drama is required. You will still need to modify your daily routine so that your main goal receives most of your resources, which most likely will adversely affect your other pursuits. But the discomfort you'll experience will be temporary. Goals get accomplished, circumstances change, and it becomes easier to identify the right priorities, that is, the priorities that improve your quality of life.

In order to contribute to your well-being your priorities should reflect your core values. You can't fake care, and chasing imposed ideals will only exacerbate your lows and insecurities. Before committing to your selected few important tasks make sure their nature and potential outcomes resonate with you (see the chapter on Values to gain clarity on this matter.) Prioritizing works only if you really care about the thing you prioritize.

Some of us may choose a hedonistic and fuzzy path of "going with the flow." While this might seem like an antidote to stress and misery, in reality, it's a clumsy attempt to cover the ugly truth — you have no idea what to do with your life. Following down this road, that is letting your life slide, will only make you perpetually dissatisfied.

Our lifetime is limited. If we want to accomplish anything worthwhile, we must manage our time mindfully. We must set priorities that support our values and follow through.

The world is full of ephemeral clamor and eternal inanity, but when we know what matters most to us, what we strive toward, and what we are willing to sacrifice for, we can handle distractions better, stay on our curated course, and that's how we can lead meaningful lives.

WRITE DOWN

your top five values*:

_____

_____

_____

_____

_____

* *You can use the ones you've established by completing exercises from the chapter on Values or revisit your values and rework the list.*

Now write down tasks you have for yourself for this week/month, noting the area to which the task belongs (health, relationships, professional growth, or personal development):

_____

_____

_____

_____

_____

_____

_____

Examine both lists and identify the areas with the most tasks. Are your top values represented by at least one task? Make sure that your task distribution aligns with your values and goals.

PRIORITIZING PRIORITIZATION

Among all the tasks you have written, create a list of your priorities for this week/month with the most important items at the top (up to five):

_____

_____

_____

_____

_____

ACTING ON ACTIONS

action (n)

the fact or process of doing something, typically to achieve an aim

- *this problem will worsen without concerted action.*

ACTING ON ACTIONS

That's a common occurrence among us: we have ambitious goals but rarely follow through on them; we talk about changing our status quo but rarely take action. We keep thinking and talking, thinking and talking, dreaming of our superior future while doing nothing new. And so we have entrepreneurs without businesses, musicians without albums, psychologists without practice, and retirees without savings. We mean to do what we believe is right and inspiring, but intentions don't equal actions. Thoughts are assumptions, actions are facts.

There are plenty of aspiring artists, sportsmen, and actors who have nothing tangible to show for it. And there are plenty of dreamers who think "that'll all work out," so they spend rather than save, envisioning themselves as the boss rather than making a business plan and relying on others for help rather than helping themselves.

It wouldn't be tragic if these individuals didn't keep believing that "the right time will come" and their aspirations would come true. By putting their lives on hold, they, that is, we, forget that we're mortal and that perfect timing may never come. It would seem that the

> *The distance between your dreams and reality is called action.*
>
> Unknown

idea of our finitude should give us urgency and determination to pursue our ambitions, but, as an abstract concept, it lacks motivational power, and so we succumb to our weaknesses, fears of failure, and the unknown.

We're afraid to face the truth: we may fail. We may not be as great of a parent or a writer or an entrepreneur as we imagined ourselves to be. As long as we keep thinking and talking, the idea that we are talented, exceptional, and full of potential is believable and heartwarming, but as soon as we get down to actions, we most likely will experience failures, and the idea of our superiority will inevitably crumble. A devastating discovery indeed.

Taking action requires confronting our fears and risking our comfortable but stagnant present, a difficult and unpleasant task in itself. To escape this discomfort, we hide behind excuses and distractions. "But I already do so much!", "But I've already done that!" — arguments we all resort to from time to time. Sure, we sacrifice a lot in the present: we keep doing tedious chores and boring work projects, we skip vacation trips to increase our savings, and we forgo delicious but unhealthy treats in favor of our health. And, for crying out loud, we read these self-help books to better understand ourselves and our circumstances, in hopes of improving our present and future. But as laudable and inspiring as our intentions may be, they don't ease the fears that prevent us from taking action.

We keep living in comfy illusions of "would" and "could" rather than experiencing sobering realities of "failed" and "gave up". Once again, there would be no problem if such betrayal of our dreams and thoughts didn't entail emotional wounds — regrets. If we didn't feel the pesky twinges of conscience that we let ourselves down, that we *missed* our opportunities, we could go on with our however mediocre lives. But we can't; we know it's not what's best for us.

> *You don't have to be great to start, but you have to start to be great.*
>
> Zig Ziglar

Some of us look back on our lives and feel weighed down by regrets, with no sense of flight. That happens when one spends too much time in the chambers of one's skull, losing sight of the fact: thoughts alone don't create a fulfilling life, their reinforcements — actions — do.

It's not to say taking action is always needed, or that it is certainly innocent and regret-free. There are times when actions hurt and cause setbacks, but that's part of their ability to bring about change, which is not always a smooth process. Progress rests on discomfort. As opposed to thoughts, which can also hurt, cause hardships and setbacks, but won't change one's life noticeably.

We need to take action if we want to finally visit that beach in that country we've been dreaming about, to finally write the novel

> **Actions prove who someone is, words just prove who they want to be.**
>
> Unknown

whose plot has been keeping us up at night, to finally monetize the hobby we've been seeing so much potential in. We need to act to make the ideas nesting in our heads a reality.

But then imagine this. You've overcome your fears and instinctive impulses to say "no". Maybe because you finally read a book that strongly resonated with you or because you attended a motivation seminar that awakened your daring self or maybe you just woke up one morning with an unwavering determination to turn over a new leaf. Inspired, you acted but didn't get the outcome you wanted. As a result, your motivation dropped, momentum was lost, and now restarting your acting engine requires tremendous effort. In fact, it takes so much effort that many of us don't even try. That's how dreams die.

It's possible to prevent this commonplace scenario by accepting two truths. First: not all actions are useful or important. There are empty actions, think of procrastination, and there are counterproductive actions, think of lying. If you want to act purposefully and efficiently, identify your values and priorities and act in accordance with them. Second: worthwhile endeavors require above-average

ACTING ON ACTIONS

strivings. If you choose a meaningful path, it's going to be a bumpy road, with motivation falling, self-doubt rising, and quitting temptations looming. Without headaches, sacrifices, and resistance, alas, nothing of significance is accomplished. Embrace this fact in advance, so when the clouds thicken and periods of apathy set in, you don't get caught off guard but are ready, calmly, to wait it out. Having strategies prepared to boost your motivation in times of need is highly recommended.

People pay thousands of dollars to attend self-help guru workshops not so much to hear something new as to get motivated, to start believing in *I can*, and get energized enough the *I do* phase. We can save ourselves money and time if we are clear on what we want and why, and identify sources of our excuses (refer to chapters on Values and Laziness). No amount of self-help books or personal growth training can improve our lives and our present unless we begin to act, and, *when* the desired results don't come, readjust our approach. Thoughts don't materialize on their own. We materialize them through our actions.

So how can you surpass the pernicious 'want' and move on to the promising 'do'? Try this: every morning when you wake up, ask yourself "*What actions will I perform today that will contribute to my X?*", X being your goal or ambition that will lead you to a brighter future, or at least a more bearable present. Then in the evening ask yourself this: "*What did I do with my precious today?*" Questions like these, which require specific answers, are uncomfortable and so aren't asked often. But it's their uncompromising and sobering nature that adds fuel to our fire, forcing us to step out of auto-pilot and take responsibility for our actions and inactions.

If this reality check isn't enough, if yet another breach of your own promise doesn't disturb you, set tangible consequences. We often procrastinate over actions because we don't see the immediate repercussions of our choices. We delude ourselves that today is insignificant and that it can be sacrificed just one more time for courting our temptations. But imagine that your house is on fire, and as you stare at your screens and keep making excuses, the fire spreads more and more with every passing day, taking away your skills, your opportunities, and your better future into oblivion. Think the fire isn't real? For all of us it's mercilessly real, otherwise we wouldn't have regrets and unfulfilled dreams. The older we get, the faster fire grows. Left unattended, it'll consume our promising future, our what-could-have-been-meaningful lives. The failure to reach for an extinguisher, that is to take actions, results in entrepreneurs without businesses, retirees without savings, and artists without artworks. And, the worst of all, regrets that cannot be rectified.

Imagine the flames, picture the destruction. What will your life look like if you keep the same pattern of actions and inactions? Make a mental picture of your tomorrow, your upcoming month, and your upcoming year. Do you like what you see? If so, great, you're living your life to the best of your

ACTING ON ACTIONS

abilities and knowledge. Don't like what you see? Be proactive or your inertia will only make matters worse.

Throughout the day, ask yourself "*What am I doing, and why?*" so that you can't hide behind a shroud of naivety and negligence. And so that you won't wake up one morning on the embers of what used to be your home and realize with pity that the life you've lived isn't yours.

The majority of our thoughts never make it into action. And frankly, not all of them should. But if you've already played out different hypotheses and scenarios, and know where you stand and what you want, get up off your bum and make your dear intentions a reality. Don't wait for an external change to make an internal change. Today is the best day to make a difference in your life both for your own sake and for the sake of those you care about. You and they will all benefit if you get your act together. Here and now.

> *Take action! An inch of movement will bring you closer to your goals than a mile of intention.*
>
> Steve Maraboli

WRITE DOWN

your goals for this month or quarter:

_____

_____

_____

_____

_____

_____

_____

_____

identify two actions that you can take this week to make progress towards each goal:

Goal 1: _____

Habit: _____

Action: _____

ACTING ON ACTIONS

Goal 2: _____
Habit: _____
Action: _____

Goal 3: _____
Habit: _____
Action: _____

Goal 4: _____
Habit: _____
Action: _____

Goal 5: _____
Habit: _____
Action: _____

Choose one of the actions you noted above to perform **today:**

_____

GRATIFYING GRATITUDE

gratitude (n)

the quality of being thankful; readiness to show appreciation for and to return kindness

- *everyday is a gift which I accept with gratitude.*

The easiest way to bring positive emotions into your everyday life is to acknowledge what you have. In other words, to be grateful. It seems like such a simple concept. It doesn't require any effort, risk, or investment. Or does it?

> *The more grateful I am, the more beauty I see.*
>
> Mary Davis

If you were to arrange things you're grateful for and things you're dissatisfied with into two piles, which one will look bigger? Which one will draw your attention first? Which one will evoke stronger emotions?

Evolution has trained us to pay greater attention to danger rather than pleasure since danger can kill us whereas pleasure doesn't have such a drastic effect. Today, even though we are way more secure, we still focus on bad things first and foremost. It happens automatically. An ingrained stubborn habit, a common pervasive behavior. Everyone complains and so we roll with it.

Appreciating what is good, however, doesn't come naturally and requires effort, sometimes even courage. Unlike criticizing, which is an act of destruction but more often is just cowardly inaction, gratitude is an active building of acceptance and trust. When we express gratitude, we put ourselves second. That's a

> *In ordinary life, we hardly realize that we receive a great deal more than we give and that it is only with gratitude that life becomes rich.*
>
> Dietrich Bonhoeffer

humble act that calls upon vulnerability. And it doesn't come easy to us, egocentric creatures.

For that very reason, we need to be mindful and remind ourselves of what makes our life easier and more enjoyable. Not wait for grand occasions to say kind words or major events to experience enthusiasm.

There are always reasons to complain: the world is unfair, people are selfish, and you don't always get what you want. There are, however, a whole lot more reasons to be thankful for. Starting from trivial sensations we take for granted — breathing, hearing, walking — and to having a hot shower and a device that lets you read these lines (and stay connected, watch pet videos, and share your humble opinion wherever you like.)

The bitter truth is that we start valuing things when we lose them. Why do we need a tragedy to see how great our lives are? How lucky are we? Right now you *are* lucky — you have time, safety, and emotional stability for such a leisurely activity as reading. But are you feeling happier now because I pointed out those things? Most likely not. You need to learn to see them for yourself if you want to become happier and more optimistic. And, let me tell you, more powerful.

For years I've deliberately practiced gratitude. I've had an evening ritual of writing down five things I was grateful for. This practice dragged me out of an apathetic, depressing hole and into an optimistic outlook. It shifted my focus from "what's wrong" to "what's good." As I practiced my gratitude journaling every day, I became more creative to avoid sounding repetitive. It felt like cheating to say "thanks for the hot shower" or "thanks that I woke up today" for days on end, so instead I trained myself to notice previously unnoticed tiny details that made a difference, like "thanks that I managed to come home right before the storm and didn't get rained on" and "thanks that when I sent a message to my mom today, her response contained a smiley face." By the way, you can address your thanks to whatever feels right for you — the Universe, God, or yourself.

Sustaining a positive state of mind made me a kinder and happier person. You can try this simple practice yourself and experience the change. Just give it a couple of weeks, so you

> *Gratitude is a currency that we can mint for ourselves, and spend without fear of bankruptcy.*

Fred De Witt Van Amburgh

> *Gratitude is not only the greatest of virtues but the parent of all others.*
>
> Marcus Tullius Cicero

can start being creative with your thanks by paying attention to finer details.

Being grateful makes you friendlier to other people. A smile, a trivial "thanks," or any other form of positive feedback will inspire and motivate others to be good and do good. Have you tried to be a jerk to nice people? It's hard. Even though sometimes it must be done (*nice* doesn't equal *innocent*). When you must be assertive, gratitude helps you stay fair and respectful and keeps you from falling into rudeness or spitefulness during mentally uncomfortable times.

Can you see now what great power you possess? You can be happier by being appreciative and you can make the world a better place by expressing your appreciation.

What are the five things you're grateful for right now? It works best when they are written down ;)

WRITE DOWN

small things that can make your daily life easier:

_____

_____
_____
_____
_____
_____
_____

Think about the people who make your life and the world a better place. Note their names below:

_____

_____

_____

_____

_____

Consider sending a thank-you message to them, acknowledging how much they mean to you.

INFINITY ON OUR FINITUDE, OR MEMENTO MORI

TRY
TRYING

try (v)

make an attempt or effort to do something

- *you could even try running every day.*

TRY TRYING

How likely are you to try a new thing? How likely are you to try again if the first encounter isn't successful? And realistically, how many attempts would you be willing to make before calling it a day?

The longer we live, the fewer new experiences we have — we've already ridden a horse, tried an Indian curry, had an acupuncture session, and so on. If we haven't had these experiences, now we're unlikely to seek them out. We're not open to new things as much, especially if this "new" can make us fall face down in the dirt, figuratively and literally. No longer are we as enthusiastic about going skating, surfing, dirt biking, taking up a new musical practice, or learning a new language as we once were. Why?

One reason is that the older we get, the more competent we think we are, and becoming a newbie again makes us feel inadequate and uncomfortable. As if we've grown out of the learning phase and now, whatever we do, we should do it right. And so, we don't take on new challenges in which we may fail and be judged. At school and work, we're not always willing to try new things and give it our all. What if we do so only to find out later that

> " *When you have exhausted all possibilities, remember this: you haven't.* "
>
> Thomas Edison

> **The greatest glory in life is not in never falling, but in rising every time we fall.**
>
> Ralph Waldo Emerson

we failed? That's a serious blow to our self-esteem, so we prefer to protect ourselves from disappointments by jumping to the conclusion: "It's not my thing." We're especially susceptible to this white-and-black evaluation of our abilities at a young age. A bad grade for an English essay can forever make us believe that we can't write, or one comment from our teacher can make us think we can't learn languages. These false beliefs can play a fateful role throughout our lives.

It's been said that those of us who are quick to give up on ourselves have a predominantly fixed mindset, which is a set of beliefs stating that our abilities are innate and can't be improved, no matter how hard we try. For example, if you catch yourself thinking while reading this book "These tips are not for me, I can't change myself" then you might have a fixed mindset. If, however, while reading these essays you thought (or better yet, wrote down), "If I change X and Y in my thinking and behavior, I can become a better person, so I'll give these practices a try," then you might have a growth mindset, the opposite to a fixed mindset: you believe you can change your abilities and, as a result, you don't give up easily.

That being said, mindset theory is relatively new, picked up by pop science, and like any theory that becomes massively popular, it's been greatly simplified and distorted. We don't have either growth or fixed mindset; they are the ends of the spectrum of how we think about ourselves. We might be venturesome in our work life — we're confident that we have valuable skills and can always make money — and, at the same time, be inhibited in our personal life — we're insecure about whether we can love or be loved. As a result, we're fine with changing jobs, but we're terrified of changing relationships, no matter how dysfunctional they are.

If you see areas in your life where you stagnate, where you think of changes but are afraid to make them, notice what thoughts block your actions and see if they are objective truths. Try to insert them in the following statement, where X is your belief and Y is your expected outcome: "100% *of people who do/have X get Y."* For example, 100% *of people who touch a hot stove get burned.* Sounds valid. And how about this: 100% *of people who ask for a promotion get a rejection.* This statement is hard to say with a straight face, isn't it? Now find examples among your family, friends, and colleagues who asked for promotions and received them. That's how you dismantle your limiting beliefs and build up the courage to ask for a raise.

If you're dissatisfied with your performance at work or school, consider how you approach the learning process. Do you put in hard work? If not, are you willing to start now? If not, why? If you find yourself saying *"I'm lazy"* or *"Now is not a good time"* or myriads of other excuses, go back to the previous paragraph and dispel those beliefs, one by one. And then when you work hard and make mistakes (oh no, who could have predicted that?), are you willing to try and fix them? And then, when needed, to try again?

The phrase "If at first you don't succeed, try, try again" is hackneyed for a reason. It reminds us to stay humble and not give up as quickly as we tend to. But how about times when you overbore your impulsiveness, and made a few attempts but saw no real progress? Maybe you didn't get what you wanted because you didn't change your approach as you tried — you repeated the same action, expecting a better result. That's Einstein's definition of insanity. The key to success is often not just to try again and again, but to try differently: harder, smarter, or both.

Rarely do we attain our desires on our first try, especially if it's a big one: getting into the university of our dreams, securing a high-paying job we enjoy, or topping a video game leaderboard. We've forgotten how many times we fell before we started walking, how many hours we spent before we acquired a new skill, how many mistakes we made before we got As, how many challenges we overcame before we landed a high-end position, and how many rounds we played before we ranked high on a leaderboard.

By forgetting the learning journey, we might think that we've always been clever and skilled, and so we should excel easily in many, if not all, things we do. Moreover, we may be intolerant of others who aren't able to do what we can, like driving or swimming, or passing a level with flying colors. Unrealistic thinking, which places high expectations on ourselves and arbitrary standards on others, hides the trap of arrogance that hinders our progress. We should watch out for this expression of a fixed mindset since it prevents us from trying harder and encouraging others to do the same.

When we keep the door to improving our abilities open, new opportunities will present themselves, along with achievements and positive emotions. But if we close the door, frightened of change and the unknown, we deprive ourselves of remarkable experiences that make life fascinating and fulfilling.

In most cases, we can debilitate or empower ourselves by how we think about difficulties — whether they are feasible or not, and this will affect how we act — we quit or we try.

Michael Jordan didn't make it to the basketball varsity team at first. But he didn't surrender. On the contrary, the following summer he trained more rigorously, improved his technique, and gained four inches in height (as if Mother Nature, impressed by his devo-

> *I'm a great believer in luck, and I find the harder I work, the more I have of it.*
>
> Thomas Jefferson

tion, also helped him grow physically). Now Michael Jordan is a basketball legend, largely because he didn't give up and stayed persistent.

This isn't a cherry-picked example. Everyone we admire or who is well-known has tried over and over again to get where they are. There's luck, of course, and talent can still play a role. But these conditions vary, unlike the universal truth we all share: the more we try, the more we achieve. So let's open our minds to trying not just new things, but also the things we failed at but want to succeed at.

WRITE DOWN

a few things you've never tried but would like to:

_____

_____

_____

_____

_____

Consider doing one of these things in the near future.

Identify one of your goals and the top three actions you believe will bring you closer to achieving it:

Goal: _____

Action: _____

Action: _____

Action: _____

Choose one of the noted actions and repeat it at least ten times. Evaluate the outcomes.

LAZILY ABOUT LAZINESS

laziness (n)

the quality of being unwilling to work or use energy; idleness

- *so again laziness becomes the mother of invention.*

Days have passed with a pizza box on the table and crumbs scattered on the floor. A growing to-do list of tasks that have been left unattended for a year. A never-ending struggle between the gym and the couch.

We all know the feeling of laziness. Whether in its extreme manifestations, such as *I don't want to do anything and leave me all alone*, and in its small nagging moments, such as *I'll do the dishes tomorrow*.

Our lives aren't disrupted by dirty dishes in the sink or work preparation put off until tomorrow and yet, postponing small and large tasks contributes to self-dissatisfaction. And because we tend to push tasks back quite often and blame ourselves for doing so, we drive ourselves into a deeper state of discontent.

At times like these, when our negative self-talk scolds us for procrastinating and we can no longer drag out our duties, we should examine the cause. Usually it's either fear or a lack of motivation.

Fear can take many forms: fear of failure, of success, of change, of rejection, of being judged, and so on. Laziness usually stems

> *Laziness is a secret ingredient that goes into failure. But it's only kept a secret from the person who fails.*
>
> Robert Half

from a fear of failure. We are afraid to perform a task that might show us that we aren't as skillful as we thought. For example, we read a self-help book and think "I can write something like this no problem!" and then when we actually sit down and write, we see that the words we've left on the page are less than satisfactory, and so each new chapter ignites resistance in us so we delay working on our book. Or our album. Or our 10K run. Often to the point of abandoning our goals completely. Our self-esteem suffered, time was spent, and the magical "tomorrow" when we performed exceptionally well never came.

Or maybe we approached our endeavors in a prudent way, dismantling illusions of easy and quick work. We predicted that certain tasks would be challenging and would make us unsatisfied with our performance, causing us to become lazy. But despite this inner preparation, the fear didn't go away and procrastination didn't stop. We keep delaying performing regardless of how wise we are. Because it's one thing to daydream and build thought castles, but quite another to face the harsh realities of our inadequate actions. Rather than confront ourselves with the possibility of failing, we avoid challenges, and until we accept the inevitability of making mistakes and having setbacks, our disinclination to act will continue.

Another source of laziness is a lack of motivation. We're not afraid to do the dishes, we just don't feel like standing in front of the sink and scrubbing away stubborn grease stains. Let's soak pans and plates yet another day, shall we?

When we can't see a benefit from accomplishing a task, we don't act. The exception is a developed habit that makes us do things automatically. To act, we need motivation. It doesn't matter whether it's reward- or fear-driven; all that matters is that it's on the forefront of our consciousness, and it's best if it's time-sensitive. Or laziness will prevail.

> *Too many young people itch for what they want without scratching for it.*
>
> Thomas Taylor

Identifying the source of your laziness will help you come up with strategies for overcoming it. If your idleness is a result of fear, you can disarm it with sound reasoning. Having doubts about your ability to succeed? But if you don't try, you won't succeed for sure. Tackling new and challenging projects is the only way to become stronger and more knowledgeable, and increase your chances for success. Feeling intimidated by others? Everyone has weaknesses and insecurities. Those you admire have been intimidated and perhaps even humiliated in public. And, believe it or not, this only contributed to their status as role models. Failure didn't stop them from trying, and persistence and a bit of luck made them who they are now. Are you worried that you won't meet the expectations of your family and friends? But what about your

> *Laziness may appear attractive, but work gives satisfaction.*
>
> Anne Frank

expectations for yourself to have a better life? Take your foot off the brake pedal and use that motivation to fuel your actions. And it's quite possible your close ones don't have the expectations you think they do.

In exposing the unfounded nature of your fears, you can overcome the inertia which comes from laziness. You realize that inaction won't get you anything worthwhile: not a better job, not a more loving relationship, not a healthier body. Hiding behind your fears ceases to be cute and safe. It may take more than one pep-talk to dismantle your inhibitions, but if you stop following them blindly, they'll lose their grip on you, and sometimes that's already enough to start acting. The same applies to excuses — they are servants of laziness. If you disarm them as you disarm your fears — revealing that your excuses don't match reality — they'll back off and give you room for action.

If your laziness is rooted in a lack of motivation, you can revive the original incentive or come up with a new one that reinvigorates you. Motivation is like meaning — it's created, not given.

Let's say you have a presentation due on Monday. You plan to finish it by the end of the week so you can enjoy the weekend with your family and friends with clear consciousness. But half of the week has passed and you haven't started working on the task. Since you have the whole weekend ahead, you think you can procrastinate a bit longer. But this thought contradicts your initial intention to relax on the weekend. If you still want to follow your original plan, visualize how nice it would be to spend time with your loved ones knowing that the task has been completed. How less stressed and more fun you'll be, and how it'll positively affect your quality time with others. The more details you imagine, the more motivated you'll feel to get this presentation out of your way. Alternatively, you can use a negative visualization technique, where you imagine how tense and anxious you'll feel having the unfinished task hanging over you. How you won't be able to enjoy your time and only dread the upcoming Monday. Considering unwanted consequences can be as motivating as considering desired ones, if not more so.

In some cases, a lack of motivation indicates that you should stop chasing things you no longer care about. As priorities and circumstances change, you'd be better off adjusting to new realities than trying to impose obsolete values on yourself. Perhaps your persistent reluctance to deliver presentations signals that you no longer want to work for that company. You've overcome your feelings of *meh* too many times to get little to no reward, and now you're not concerned about whether or not the presentation goes well, whether you will be praised or criticized. You've lost your "*why*" and procrastination is there to highlight the loss. If you can't find or recreate your drive, if you no longer can see the point of working for that company or finishing that task, it might be time to move on. Not every abandonment is a defeat; sometimes it's exactly what you need to win. Just don't rush serious decisions. Mood changes affect your reasoning as well, so take time to make sure your acedia isn't the result of low blood sugar or unrelated frustration but rather of unfulfilling pursuits.

And let's not forget that we are all human and sometimes laziness is just the body's way of indicating that our physiological needs aren't being met. A good night's sleep and a balanced meal can often be all we need to snap out of inertia.

In cases where visualizing rewarding scenarios, dismantling your fears, or treating yourself with your favorite food do nothing or make you feel worse, there might be more serious reasons behind your laziness, such as depression or burnout. If you stop feeling enthusiastic about the things you used to enjoy and if no reward seems appealing, consider talking to your friends or seeing a doctor to dig deeper into your mental state. An outside perspective can be eye-opening.

A certain amount of laziness will always be present in our life. We can't like and be enthusiastic about everything all the time. But when laziness is a recurring theme, examining our "*why*" — why we want to do what we're unwilling to do now — can help us adjust our life's compass so that it points towards more actions and fewer excuses.

WRITE DOWN

a few things that you are always happy to do:

_____

_____

_____

_____

For each item, identify a reward that you get from doing those things.

Circle the rewards and explore ways to incorporate them into tasks to motivate yourself to do things that you may not want to do but know you should.

UNBORING BOREDOM

bored (adj)

feeling weary and impatient because one is unoccupied or lacks interest in one's current activity

- *they hung around all day, bored stiff.*

I hear the phrase "I'm bored" far too often nowadays. We, modern people, who have so many entertainment options, who carry a bottomless supply of amusement and knowledge in our pockets, who have access to what none of the generations before had — pet videos, stand-up comedy recordings, true crime podcasts — are getting bored easily and frequently. And what's worse, we're afraid of boredom more than ever.[1]

> *Boredom is simply the lack of an interesting perspective.*
>
> Brooke Noel Moore

Boredom is that annoying feeling that colors life into dull, tedious shades. It's an unpleasant state of low arousal that we yearn to be rid of. What's there, in ennui, anyway? Why do we get bored and what purpose does it serve? Philosophers and scientists are on a quest to uncover these mysteries, and while those questions remain relatively unanswered, we have gained deeper insights. If you'd like to learn more about four types of boredom[2] or five[3] that science defines today, please follow the footnotes.

For the sake of simplicity, I'll turn to Heidegger[4] here (said no one ever, and yet...). He classifies boredom into three types[5]: being bored by something, being bored with something, and profound boredom. These types will help us identify boredom and figure out how to treat it.

An example of being bored by something would be waiting in a line, or at a bus stop, or at the end of that terrible movie that seemed to last forever. When we don't like what we experience, we turn to distractions to make the time pass. But distractions are rarely fulfilling and meaningful, especially in retrospect.

Being bored with something is similar to the previous type, except that it's not caused by an external event but by our perception of it. We went to the party and it seemed decent, but in the aftermath we think of it as boring and regret wasting time there. We gained no fulfillment, just disappointment. Heidegger regards both of these types of boredom as superficial.

In contrast, Heidegger believes that the third type, "profound boredom," can lead us to authenticity. Usually experienced in lonely moments, it arises from a sense that "something is missing." While we can't pinpoint exactly what's missing, the feeling makes us search for a lost piece of the puzzle. Even if no answers are found, searching stimulates our minds and may inspire new solutions. There is scientific evidence that this type of boredom makes our creative juices flow[6].

It's the superficial kinds I'm worried about[7]. The ones that are unappealing and unproductive; that unapologetically rob us of our precious lifetime; the ones that are companions of depression, coloring the world into greys and framing it with apathy. These types of boredom cause us to like our lives less, which is tragic since we only have so much time to enjoy being alive.

Is there a way to turn the mundane into profound? To see the fascinating new in the dull old? To appreciate a slow pace? To revel in seemingly simple experiences? To be less bored and more satisfied? I believe there is.

There are three practices that worked for me and I believe they'll work for you, too, if you give them a chance.

Building up awareness.

As we become more aware of our judgments and feelings, we are able to shift our attention, resulting in more positive experiences. Boredom isn't something that happens to us, it's something we create. It's not the experiences themselves that are boring, but how we perceive them. Exactly because of that, we hold more power over them. You've probably heard the saying "if you can't change your feelings, change your attitude." However hard that may be, it is possible. The same is true with boredom — you can transform a dull ac-

> *Boredom is the feeling that everything is a waste of time; serenity, that nothing is.*

Thomas Szasz

tivity into an engrossing adventure. It might not always work, though. In fact, it's more likely to fail than to work, especially in the beginning, but with more practice, more wonders of your mind will emerge and "boring" will transform into "enriching." The hyped meditation is back once again to help us be here, to be attentive and present. Follow your breath or the shimmering of your closed eyes, or repeat an affirmation to declutter your mind.

Exercising self-control.

For boredom that we experience due to the lack of stimulation, when social media, TV shows, games, and podcasts fail to deliver that avidly eager surge of dopamine, we can blame only ourselves. We are never satiated with the media. If we'd like to be less reliant on screens to cheer us up, we must wean ourselves from endless consumption. Otherwise, our demand for entertainment will continue to rise, making it increasingly difficult to leave us satisfied. Even the billions of transistors in our phones can't rid us of boredom. Only our conscious efforts can.

And here comes the buzzword "detox." Make a habit of sitting by yourself in silence and just be. Start with as little as one minute and gradually increase it to 10 minutes or more each day. It's not meditation; you can think about whatever you please. Just no props: no screens, no books, no headphones. Entertain, or dull yourself, with the only tool in your possession: your brain.

Igniting curiosity.

There's so little we know about the world around us and about ourselves. There's always so much to discover, so much to observe. Hackneyed things can be seen in a completely new light if we're open to examining them closer. We need to keep asking questions without relying on our preconceived notions to find answers, without a hope to find any answers at all. What, how, and why can turn even the dullest things into an exciting discovery.

While typing the previous paragraph, I lost concentration due to fatigue and turned to a stingy feeling in my thumb. I spotted a thread of cuticles that stood perpendicular to my fingernail. Out of habit, I began to wonder why that piece of skin had a special name; what it was made of; whether it contained molecules from the pizza I ate some time ago; how long it could grow like this before I ripped it out. I didn't Google those questions, and I'll never find out the answer to the last one because I don't have the patience to walk around with my cuticle turned up like that. But what happened is this: I became engaged with being alive, in whatever quirky way. That kind of boredom pulled me closer to life, not further away. It also served as a reset button, giving me a much-needed break.

All three of these practices are intertwined, as you can see. They stem from being here and now. Being attentive. Being open to new information. Try them yourself to see how annoying boredom can be turned into a rewarding experience.

> *Boredom is an insult to oneself.*
>
> Jules Renard

Next time you stand in line, look around instead of looking at your phone (however tempting it may be). You don't necessarily need to force yourself to make up stories about the people around you — who they are, how they got here, or what the hell all of them forgot there at that very moment when you need to do your thing fast. It can be mentally draining, and you might not be in the mood for it. But simply look at the situation as something different than what you are used to.

You can imagine looking at the line from above and seeing yourself as just one link in the crooked chain in which you were temporarily entangled. How many links are there? How much space is there between people? How will a person in front of you react if you stare at their neck or take a step closer? (And that's how you're now conducting a field study of "the psychic staring effect.")

Or maybe you turn to the ground, looking at your shoes like you never looked at them before. Where do the materials of your shoes come from? What number of people were involved in making and distributing these shoes? How would it feel to stand here barefoot without shoes and feel the cold carpet tiles underneath? (And that's how you could start getting weird looks.) Your mind will wander and ask questions effortlessly. All you need to do is to nudge it a bit first and then it will lead you to all sorts of surprising places, aka a Wikipedia search without Wikipedia.

Or let's say you go to the movies with your friends. The film is a bust, you're bored, and you'd rather leave, but your friends insist on staying. You can do damage control by picturing how this yet-to-be failure was created. How a board of very important people — directors, actors, and producers — sat at a big table, approving that nonsensical, lazily, and cruelly written script, and how the majority of them agreed to put time and money into making that disaster (what on earth were they thinking?) How a director, assistant director, 2nd assistant director, camera assistant, camera operator, videographer, best boy, gaffer — the list goes on — were all on a movie set doing their best — or not so much — to create the illusion of reality only to have failed in such a boring way. Or how actors forgot their lines or had a slip of a tongue, and then the whole crew cracked up frenetically. (The best time to picture that laughing fit is during what were supposed to be dramatic or terrifying moments.) And here you are, relaxing on a comfy couch taking on the role of a captious critic.

And if there's nothing to hold onto — no people, no moving pictures, no feelings — you're stuck, waiting, and bored out of your mind, you still can turn that monotony around and benefit from it.

I know that trees with their hundreds of thousands of unique leaves don't please the eyes and the fact that we stand still while the Earth rotates at a speed of 1,000 miles per hour in a 200 billion trillion-star universe doesn't give us a toss. But how about turning inward and tuning to the processes that sustain our lives? Your heart pumps 1.3 gallons of blood, your lungs process 4 gallons of air, your neurons pass 86 billion electrical signals, all that within the span of a single minute! I know these are just numbers that cease to fascinate (the higher the number, the more abstract it gets, and the less impressive it is perceived). But you can fish for weird sensations in your body that are always different, always changing, and thus engaging. The eyelids of closed eyes that are always trembling, never still; the heartbeat echoing in your rib cage, in your skull, in the tips of your toes (you can feel that throbbing reaching all the way down if you care to feel); the weight on your spine and the pain of the trapezius muscle. I'm pampered by the fact that I'm living. Are you? Just imagining, or rather trying to imagine how busy our bodies work is enough to keep us entertained when the mundanity of washing dishes or waiting in traffic catches up with us. If you tried this practice and didn't find it helpful, you at least lowered your blood pressure[8] and increased your heart rate variability[9], both are linked with good health.

Now I rarely get bored. To bore me, you'd have to make me sit through a monotonous lecture led by a professor who's sick of doing it and strangle me with a dryly written textbook. But even then, I sense that if only I had the mental capacity to understand the lecture and the textbook, I would appreciate the complexity of the delivered material and not watch the clock.[10]

I learned to appreciate what I would be unlikely to appreciate before. Now I'm not bored when I watch a lengthy movie (let's see a show of hands who watched "Gone with the Wind" in one sitting without nodding off). I'm not bored when I watch a slow-paced movie ("Roma" would only benefit from being longer, in my humble opinion). I'm not bored even when I watch the "best of both worlds" — the lengthy, slow-paced "Lawrence of Arabia." (Who knew that a nearly four-hour film in a desert could be so fascinating?)

I'm not bored when I'm alone. I feel completely fine even in a dark quiet room with no screens. That's not because I have a rich inner world — though I wish I did! And I don't fill my lack of stimulation with deep thoughts or creative ideas. I don't make up stories or fantasize or dream. Nor do I constantly worry about something or plan what I am going to do next weekend. All of these mental activities can obscure boredom. But what works

> **When you pay attention to boredom, it gets unbelievably interesting.**
>
> Jon Kabat-Zinn

for me best, what makes me always engage with the world, is awareness. My brain notices so many things that I don't, so there's always something to be surprised by.

I believe practicing awareness, developing self-control, and exercising curiosity allowed me to dive deeper into sensory and rational cognition and broaden my perceptions and thinking. And there's no superficial boredom in this fascinating world of thoughts and feelings, in being here and now.

Now I see there are no "boring" experiences per se, it is only our perception of them that makes them such. Remember that you have an opportunity, the power to turn even the dullest of things into a profound experience. Which, in turn, will make you an exciting individual. And don't get me started on the notion of "boring people." As everything can be fascinating, everything can also get boring, so I'm signing off.

Happy un-boring!

WRITE DOWN

activities that feel like a burden or drain your energy:

_____

_____

_____

_____

_____

_____

_____

_____

Find or create an opportunity to experience those things while being fully present in the moment. Pay attention to every detail, and approach them with curiosity and openness. Maybe you'll notice something unusual, odd, or funny - anything can become an enriching experience if you want it to be.

RESPECTING SELF-RESPECT

respect (n)

a feeling of deep admiration for someone or
• *something elicited by their abilities, qualities,
or achievements.*

RESPECTING SELF-RESPECT

There are times when we determine our self-worth — whether we like ourselves or not — based on snippets of our behavior: we made a mistake, we helped a stranger, we were rude, we solved a problem, we made a donation, we betrayed a friend's trust, etc. And we conclude, sometimes as often as a few times a day depending on how volatile our self-esteem is, whether we are good people or not. Such a wobbly approach to valuing oneself leads to personal insecurities and poor decisions.

Our view of ourselves can be stabilized by developing self-respect, which isn't easily swayed by steep thoughts because it's based on observable principles and sequential actions. If we want to develop integrity, have a healthy self-esteem that helps us succeed in both our professional and personal lives, and be surrounded by decent people, we need to pay attention to how we treat ourselves. When we are self-respectful, we act according to our values and priorities without feeling apologetic, indecisive, or regretful, without doubting ourselves, and without letting others deem us insignificant or dupable. We set boundaries and nurture our

> *If you want to be respected by others, the great thing is to respect yourself. Only by that, only by self-respect will you compel others to respect you.*
>
> Fyodor Dostoyevsky

needs. This all contributes to a more fulfilling and satisfying life.

At work, self-respect makes us more productive — we are confident enough to close the door and pause checking emails so we can better focus on our tasks rather than reacting to seemingly urgent matters that, one would argue, don't provide as much value as concentrated work. Having self-respect also helps us maintain a healthy work-life balance — we take breaks and keep a realistic, manageable workflow, so we don't overwork ourselves into burnout. And we stop seeing our mistakes as a reflection of our worth but rather as a source of learning and growth.

In interpersonal relationships, self-respect is just as important. By setting our boundaries, we can guard ourselves against frustrations, grudges, and offenses as well as avoid being exploited by others. We're better able to spot disrespectful behavior from others and cut it in the bud before it adversely affects our relationship and our self-worth.

When we respect ourselves, we take better care of our needs and pay more attention to the needs of others. When we respect our time, we're more likely to respect other people's time since we understand, firsthand, how valuable time is and why being late or failing to communicate effectively is bad. When we respect our space, we're more likely to respect other people's space, and thus walking in without knocking or rearranging another's belongings is unacceptable to us. I say "more likely" because there's still a possibility that some of us are hypocrites who expect others to give them what they don't give themselves. Such behavior is fraught with the loss of friends and social connections — no healthy relationships can exist without reciprocity.

To respect yourself, you must be intimately familiar with your virtues and weaknesses. List the qualities you value in other people and the qualities that irritate you in them. Which of these traits do you possess? You're most likely to notice in others what you already have in yourself or what you have strong emotional attachments to. Use those qualities as stepping stones to building self-respect: cherish the ones you like and be aware of those you don't.

Let's say you respect people who keep their word, the "said-done" conduct. Daily life gives you plenty of opportunities to see if you're keeping your word. If yes, it's a solid underpinning to your foundation of self-respect: acknowledge it to give it weight. If not, take notice when you don't follow through and try to amend your ways. Simple changes, such as promising to return a call and actually doing so, are the first steps in the right direction. The more you follow through with your commit-

> *Your relationship with yourself sets the tone for every other relationship you have.*
>
> Robert Holden

ments, the easier it'll be to follow through on your commitment to follow through, making you more reliable and respectful.

Or let's say you get annoyed when someone interrupts you. Consider first whether you yourself often interrupt others. You might have developed this habit as a child — you weren't taught to wait patiently for others to finish their sentences and now you talk over other people without even realizing it. Or perhaps it's an indication that you're not interested in other people's ideas and opinions. Either way, you must be aware of your ineffective behavior in order to change it.

Ensure that you always have a clear answer to the question "*What grounds do I have for self-respect?*" so that you can make shrewd decisions in difficult situations rooted in your strengths, not your weaknesses.

It doesn't suffice to build your self-respect, you also have to communicate it to the outside world effectively so that others know what you can and can't tolerate, and behave accordingly. And even then, ambiguities rise and further clarifications are needed. Suppose you always wanted to be monogamous, but your partner suggests an open relationship. You're not willing to accept it, so you have to clarify your position. Self-worth makes it easier to advocate your stance and be firm while doing so: you don't cave in to your partner's equivocal arguments, you don't adhere to values that aren't yours, and you don't give in to appeals to emotion. Thus, regardless of the outcome of that difficult conversation, your conscience is clear: you didn't betray yourself.

A strong sense of self-respect, however, can have a downside — we set a behavioral moral bar too high for others to reach, meaning we get disappointed more often. We can also get too arrogant and cross the line between healthy self-respect and narcissism. Even though the two are different, one isn't really the continuation of the other, chances are that frequent witnessing of others' behaviors that lack strong ethics and ethos we've learned to value can turn us into disdainful snobs. There's an easy reality check: *are there people in your life who will support you at any time of day and night? And are you willing to do the same for them?* If the answer is "yes," then you are unlikely to be an arrogant strut and should encourage a sense of self-respect not only in yourself but in your friends and family.

When we respect ourselves, we're less susceptible to manipulation. When we respect ourselves, we can clearly say "no" when we believe it's the right answer. When we respect ourselves, we act in accordance with our values, making the right choice and feeling good about ourselves.

Our morale is stronger and our satisfaction with ourselves and our relationships is higher. The ability to respect ourselves allows us to live the life we want and be around people we like. Isn't that enough of a reason to consider paying respect to your self-respect?

WRITE DOWN

qualities you like about yourself. Don't be shy:

_____

_____

_____

_____

_____

qualities you like in other people:

_____

_____

_____

_____

_____

_____

_____

actions you take or would like to take to support the listed qualities above:

___

___

___

___

___

___

___

Do you have any personal principles that you follow? For instance, "keep your promises", "be truthful", or "support your friends". Write them down below and refer to them whenever you face a difficult decision.

_____

_____

_____

_____

_____

_____

_____

PROMISING PROMISES

promise (n)

a declaration or assurance that one will do something or that a particular thing will happen

• *I wanted proof, not promises.*

We've all been there. We make a promise we know we're unlikely to keep. Or worse — we can't keep. For some absurd reason, we use the fact that we can't control everything as an excuse for our improper behavior.

> "A promise is a commitment to perform. It is not a wish."
>
> M. J. Ryan

We say we'll be there on time even when we're running late and physically can't cover X distance in Y time. We say we'll return borrowed money to a friend when our paycheck has been spent and we don't have enough to cover the rent. We say we'll help our colleague with their presentation when we've already made other plans for that evening. And why, for heaven's sake, do we have to do other people's jobs? But we promised. No matter how many excuses we come up with, they can't justify the fact that we can betray someone's trust.

Naturally, we don't want to break our promises and yet, if we're not vigilant, we keep doing it. We neglect the importance of our word. We undermine other people's respect for us. Why do we keep fooling ourselves and others when it clearly doesn't do any good? I think this self-deception stems from insecurity and fear of responsibility. And, to make

> *Promises are the currency of trust.*
>
> Unknown

matters worse, our immaturity clashes with our ego that has a hard time admitting our limitations and inabilities.

Breaking promises is a path to mediocrity. You deceive yourself enough on a daily basis. At least when you give promises, think about whether you want to keep them and if you can, as well as how you'll feel about yourself if you don't follow through.

Have some standards for yourself. Hold yourself accountable for your words and you'll most likely become a stronger person. And, as a bonus, people will want to do business with you.

WRITE DOWN

promises you made to yourself and broke:

_____

_____

_____

promises you made to yourself and kept:

_____

_____

_____

promises you made to others and broke:

_____

_____

_____

promises you made to others and kept:

_____

_____

_____

promises you have now for yourself and others:

_____

_____

_____

In which of the lists do you think they will end up?

PROMISING PROMISES

ACCEPTING REJECTION

rejection (n)

the dismissing or refusing of a proposal, idea, etc.

- *singles stay single trying to avoid rejection.*

ACCEPTING REJECTION

You probably know the feeling when you meet someone and, before you even get a good look at them or speak to them, you already dislike them. And you've probably experienced the opposite: even before talking to a person, you want to get to know them better. Love at first sight, if it exists, would be an extreme example of such an occurrence.

We form impressions of people within seconds. Unconsciously, we judge others by their appearance, including their facial features and clothes, their body odor, and the circumstances in which we receive all these signals. Moreover, we don't even need to see a person to form our opinion about them. We can dislike a person apriori based on reasons unrelated to his or her character: communication circumstances (think of calling a tax office), our moods (think of displaced anger), or others' opinions (think of gossip). In these situations, the person will have a harder time winning our favor, and we'll be more likely to reject or be rude to him or her. The only exception is when we meet a person of higher social status and/or greater wealth that we're willing to reconsider our initial verdicts. In

> *You have to know how to accept rejection and reject acceptance.*
>
> Ray Bradbury

most cases, though, we are quick to lump people into those we favor and those we dislike, rarely giving them an opportunity to prove us wrong.

This categorization is often based solely on our superficial assumptions, which are deceptive and can be easily manipulated. Do you want to look more successful? Put on a tailored suit. Do you want to appear smarter? Look into your interlocutor's eyes, preferably through thick glasses. We like and dislike people not because of who they are, but because we think we know who they are. People's appearance, smell, and environment don't necessarily reflect their personalities, and yet we operate as they do. A little information, however unreliable, is better than no information at all.

If you observe yourself, the way you react to strangers, the way you see them and sort them into your mental pockets — an annoying twat, a cool guy, a greedy ghoul, a good soul — you'll be amazed at how uncompromising you can be. And how easy and painless the labeling process is. We don't have to feel active anger or have justified objections for someone to refuse or ignore them. But when we are rejected by others, we take it as a personal attack. Rejection hurts us deeply. A door slammed in our faces, literally and figuratively, hits our sense of dignity hard and if we have shaky self-esteem, it can make us feel insecure and inferior.

All of us have experienced rejection because it's such a common act. We say "no" and refuse others' ideas, offers, and even personalities constantly. And how can we not? We are limited

ACCEPTING REJECTION

in time and attention, so saying "yes" to everything would make it impossible for us to accomplish anything worthwhile. Imagine how much time you would have to implement your plans and achieve your goals if you always said yes to everyone. Very little to no at all, I dare say.

Our acceptance or rejection of others has often more to do with us than with them. Today we refused to help our parents because we had our own plans but we promised to help them on the weekend. Yesterday we snapped at a waiter because we were in a bad mood but today we smiled at their colleague as a way to atone for yesterday's rudeness. When we see how our rejection of others often has nothing to do with them, that they aren't the cause of our negative behavior but our problems, moods, and unconscious instincts are, we become more adept at handling the rejections we receive.

There are instances, however, when rejections have a clear rationale. We don't get promoted because we don't perform well, we don't get a mortgage because we have a low credit score, or our manuscript doesn't get accepted because it's badly written. All these "no's" are signals that our behavior doesn't meet accepted norms, and if we still intend to succeed, we need to reconsider our approach. A well-founded "no" is a cue, feedback guiding us to change so we can improve or exercise our creativity to find new ways to reach our goals.

Justified or not, rejections are painful. Spending much time online — a hostile and judgemental environment — doesn't help the problem. There we can get rebuffed dozens, if not

> *Rejection is an opportunity for your selection.*
>
> Bernard Branson

hundreds, of times daily — a lack of likes, a surplus of dislikes and insults, caustic comments, and cyberbullying. It would seem that after being rejected so frequently, we should've grown a hard shell around our egos. Yet just one quip can ruin our mood and cause a number of mental problems (especially in teenagers).

When we share our thoughts, ideas, and creative works online, we put ourselves in a vulnerable position. We voluntarily expose ourselves to judgment from others, and often in a virtual space, without eye contact, without serious repercussions, this judgment is harsh. We seek validation from others and if the feedback we wished for is not there, our self-acceptance suffers severely. It can get to the point that we don't accept ourselves unless we are accepted by others. *How many likes did I receive? Did I make a fool of myself by sharing that photo or writing that tweet?* We seek a benchmark, a measurement, a way to compare and define our worth. We allow others to control what we see as failure and success, important and worthless.

Do you think you are immune to it? Imagine you receive one hundred likes within a minute. How does it make you feel? Now imagine you get one hundred dislikes within a minute. Depending on social feedback, you feel differently about yourself and a piece of virtual data you put out. There are two of you now. One is elevated, and the other is miserable. One feels empowered, and the other one wants to crawl under the blanket. One wants to keep going and the other wants to give up. Again, such extremes are more common among younger people, but even those of us who boldly declare, "I don't care what anyone says about me," will no doubt notice likes and read comments and have a change in mood one way or the other.

It takes resilience, self-confidence, and wisdom to stay true to your values and beliefs regardless of external evaluation. Unfortunately, these qualities of a strong character are forged over time, and not learned from self-help books. The older we get, the less prefrontal cortex activity we have and the less cortisol (the stress hormone) is released when we're being watched[1]. In other words, as we age, we worry less about what other people think of us. But that doesn't mean we become immune to rejection. As social animals, we are wired to seek acceptance from others, so acts of rejection rarely go unnoticed.

Making peace with the reality that there are people who resent us takes time and practice. Yes, even you, however angelic you believe yourself to be. There are people out there who dislike you, no matter the validity of their reasons. You know it's the case because you yourself resent some individuals, either

> **We all learn lessons in life. Some stick, some don't. I have always learned more from rejection and failure than from acceptance and success.**
>
> Henry Rollins

unjustly or rightfully. My mom used to say, "You're not a $100 bill everyone likes," the liberating truth. Everyone is subject to contempt from others, and there's nothing special about being rejected. It's the norm. I can't name any person that everyone likes or any piece of art or scientific discovery that everyone appreciates. Can you? If you could think of an example, then go online and search "X is bad" where X is whatever you think is beyond criticism. You'll likely be surprised by the spitefulness you'll witness.

Knowing that everyone experiences rejection, noticing how you yourself reject others, and appreciating the fact that nothing has a 100% approval rate helps to deal with the pain of being rejected. It doesn't make the pain go away completely — evolution wired us otherwise — but it opens up a possibility to see a rejection as a lesson and overcome it quicker. Whatever happens, the ultimate judge of you and your behavior is you. You should live a life that makes you less likely to deny yourself, and that's what this book is written for, especially the chapters on values and self-respect.

WRITE DOWN

people you don't want to spend time with:

_____

_____

_____

When you reject someone, do you believe that they are malicious or wicked, or do you simply not like them? Or perhaps the circumstances you find yourself in push you away from them?

Your rejection of them doesn't make them bad people. Similarly, if someone rejects you, it's most likely not about you, but about them and their circumstances.

List situations where you found yourself saying "no" to people or things. Reflect on whether these refusals were based on a genuine dislike of the person or thing, or whether they stemmed from your own personal preferences at that specific time and place.

_____

_____

_____

_____

_____

_____

Rejection is a universal experience. Sometimes you reject, and sometimes you are rejected. It is an important part of life, as every "no" is a tool that makes room for what truly aligns with your goals and values.

ACCEPTING REJECTION

REGRETTING REGRET

regret (n)

a feeling of sadness, repentance, or disappointment over an occurrence or something that one has done or failed to do

- *my intention was to minimize my future regret.*

REGRETTING REGRET

No matter how sensible we are, some of our decisions and actions are bound to become regrets. Even the best-intentioned and seemingly bulletproof choices can upset us since they are always made without certain knowledge of the future. Probability and randomness, along with luck or lack thereof, can leave even the most stoic of us to stay awake at night wondering why things turned out the way they did and whether our present would be any better if we had done things differently.

In young adulthood, the weight of regret, if there's any, is light. After all, there're still so many opportunities to rectify our missteps. As time passes, however, the burden feels heavier and we're more prone to dwell on bitter memories and unfortunate circumstances because we know on some level that the future isn't always rosy, time wanes, and life doesn't get any fairer. This truth along with accumulated emotional scars can deform our present and stifle our future if we remain trapped in *what if* and *if only*.

We mentally torture ourselves by picturing hypothetical scenarios about the past that, for whatever reason, usually lead to a better pres-

> *Regret for the things we did can be tempered by time; it is regret for the things we did not do that is inconsolable.*
>
> Sydney J. Harris

ent than we have now. *Had I only asked her out / invested in Bitcoin / didn't drive that night, we think, then my marriage would have been happy / I would be a millionaire / I wouldn't have been convicted.* Thinking in this manner is similar to daydreaming, albeit twisted — there is no possibility that these scenarios can ever come true. The past is not subject to the subjunctive mood. Yet, we continue to envision lucky scenarios because they trick us, even if only for a spare second, that we could have it better than we do. But then, when we come back to reality and face an unfavorable contrast, we become bitter and anxious. Is there another way to approach regrets that can improve our mental state rather than worsen it?

Any thought process can be immensely useful if it is purposeful. If you switch to pondering your failings in a spiral manner rather than a habitual circle one, you can get to their cores and learn from them. Sadness and repentance are clues that something is off and needs to be addressed, especially if these negative feelings have become thorns in your mind. To pull them out, ask pointed questions for insight and relief.

Let's say it's been weeks, months, or even years and you still mourn your last relationship. Or your past job. Or your decision to move abroad. Occasionally you reminisce about the good old days and regret that that person, job, or place that brought you so much joy isn't a part of your life anymore. Now let's stop this hackneyed grieving for a moment and bring in some fresh air — a fact that memory distorts. Memory tends to simplify and exaggerate what happened in the past, so you're probably not telling yourself the true story. Why did that relationship end? Why did you quit that job? Why did you move to another country? There has likely been a reason for your action, and not necessarily an innocent or random one. There could have been conflicts of interest and values that affected your choices. There could have been a lack of information and experience that led to undesirable outcomes. There could have been and most likely were so many variables that you had and didn't have control over that now you can only appreciate the complexity of what your past self endured. That unformed person you were didn't know what you know now, didn't have the experience you have now, and naturally struggled to make sense of what and why happened. Hindsight makes it easy to judge or victimize, but awareness of what your past self was going through makes your present self more understanding and wiser.

You can lower the weight of your regrets by reflecting on the circumstances, priorities, and goals that surrounded those events you now feel bad about. Given what you knew and had back then, could you have made better choices? If yes, now you have first-hand experience of what *not* to do and are equipped to make smarter decisions in similar circumstances. If not, let it sink in that ignorance, unfairness, and luck are a part of life, and be tolerant of your past actions that turned out to be mistakes.

Reflecting on the past and analyzing regrets should have a purpose: improving, becoming smarter, and letting go of be-

> *To regret one's own experiences is to arrest one's own development. To deny one's own experiences is to put a lie into the lips of one's own life. It is no less than a denial of the soul.*
>
> — Oscar Wilde

liefs that keep you from moving forward. Let's look at another example of regret that sabotages your life. Say you wish you went to that university or worked for that company. You think you could have achieved much more *if only*. There may be some truth in your reasoning — you may have been more successful if you had taken the steps you hadn't. But the belief that you'd definitely be better off is false. You can't know for sure how things would have turned out. But what you can know is that you are dissatisfied with your present. Try to understand underlying reasons — what makes you come back to thinking about the missed opportunities of a better education and a higher-paid job? Is it a lack of wealth, recognition, or something else you define as "success"? What is missing from your present and what do you think you can do about it? Hint: You definitely can do something about it, and how you view potential solutions and obstacles shows whether you're ready to move forward or are stuck in the past. If you keep crying over spilled milk, you mercilessly deprive yourself of a happier present and future. That is pointless, to put it mildly, and defeats the purpose of regrets — to help us learn and grow.

Brooding on our regrets can be paralyzing. We can become fearful of making decisions after seeing what deplorable outcomes they may produce. (That is, ironically, one of the main sources of regret: missed opportunities due to fear and indecision.) But we are all in the same boat. Every one of us lives without complete information, without guarantees for tomorrow, and without coverage for mistakes. In such a fragile state, all we can do is learn to trust ourselves and proceed with caution.

Make your decisions based on the best information you have at the time. And acknowledge this fact so that your future self won't have a claim on your past self. Make a mental note that you tried to do the right thing and applied your analytical skills to the fullest. (If you rely more on intuition and emotions, remember that they are fickle and it's desirable to combine them with rationality in decision-making.) Yet no matter how hard you try, chances are beyond your control, and just by living and choosing you are always at risk, to a greater or lesser extent. Even the brainiest and most prudent of us have their list of regrets.

It's helpful to read other people's regrets to accept their ubiquitous, inevitable, and painful nature. Numerous websites exist where individuals share their pangs of guilt and heaviness of heart publicly and anonymously. You may be surprised to learn that your regrets aren't so unique. Patterns will emerge — remorse for unfair treatment of loved ones, being too shy or too harsh, neglecting the innermost, and holding onto the harmful. You will see that other people have had similar situations and made similar mistakes as you and that they experience sleepless nights and low spirits for similar reasons. As a spectator, not a protagonist of these stories, you'll be able to see that self-blame is often unwarranted and counterproductive, so you may learn to let go of your own torments.

Reading other people's regrets can also give you an idea of what you may regret in the future. For instance, you probably don't realize how rarely you call your parents. But becoming aware that such behavior is a common cause of regrets — *I wish I could call my mom and hear her say "everything is gonna be alright" and I wish I could call my dad and tell him how my day went* — will make you dial them up and maybe even appreciate that they answer your call. While this approach doesn't guarantee regret-free living, your future self will suffer less and cope with life's vicissitudes better.

You can even go a step further and use a technique the Stoics called Negative Visualization. Flip your What Ifs around — instead of feeling disappointed over something that has happened or been done, be grateful for something that hasn't happened and is not the case. Take a closer look at your present — a great deal of loss and pain can befall you at any time. You could go to the kitchen to get a cup of coffee but slip along the way, fall, and break a limb. Or you could knock over a cup of coffee on your electronics and knock out a thousand or more bucks in a second. Or you could just drop a cup on the floor and waste time looking for shards that you'd later accidentally cut yourself on. Such acts of visualizing adverse scenarios can teach us to appreciate the fact that, for all the possibilities of screwing up, we're still keeping afloat and can even enjoy a cup of coffee.

You could go one step further and imagine your life without a home, loved ones, and many other things that make your life easier, more enjoyable, and more meaningful. Although such an act might be mentally challenging, it serves as a reminder of the truth: things can always get worse. Always.

Regrets can help us improve our decision-making process. A warning sign for adjusting our life strategy, they offer valuable insight into how not to behave. By examining our past and present, we can better understand our sorrows and avoid making the same mistakes again in the future. Accepting that we can never know anything for sure will ease the process of letting go of past wrongs and forgiving ourselves.

To live is to stumble, and to move forward we must learn to rid ourselves of the dead burden of regret, replacing it with wisdom.

> *A man is not old until his regrets take the place of his dreams.*
>
> John Barrymore

WRITE DOWN

The regrets you might have when looking back on your life:

_____

_____

_____

_____

Identify the daily actions that contribute to those regrets, and then determine ways to eliminate or modify those actions to reduce the likelihood of experiencing those regrets:

_____

_____

_____

_____

_____

_____

_____

_____

INFINITY ON OUR FINITUDE, OR MEMENTO MORI

death (n)

the permanent ending of vital processes in a cell or tissue

• *his early death was a great loss to science.*

INFINITY ON OUR FINITUDE, OR MEMENTO MORI

We live and others die. It's always been like this for us and we can't imagine how it could be otherwise. We're used to hearing the news of "a dozen people died in an accident" and not thinking much about it. Death has become a hackneyed plot twist in TV and books, and an entertaining action in video games, numbing our sensitivity to the end of others' existence. When someone we know dies, we exclaim "*What?! They died??! I can't believe it! They were so young!* (or *I just talked to him/her yesterday!* or *He/she was getting better!*"). We experience grave emotions, from mild sadness to total shock, and yet a part of us accepts the news and sighs with relief: "*Once again, another human dies, but not I. Never I.*" It's the normal course of things.

In our minds, we know that death will come to us one day, but living keeps us from genuinely believing this truism. Sometimes, at night, The Arzamas Horror[1] can come over us and in a cold sweat we wonder what it would be like to cease to exist. But since our imagination cannot encompass what we virtually know nothing about, our minds create a barrier between speculation and actual ex-

> " Finiteness is an essential feature of human life, reminding us to make the most of the time we have. "
>
> Irvin D. Yalom

BE YOUR OWN GURU

> *You never know how much time you have left, but you can choose how you want to spend it.*
>
> Charles Bukowski

perience. We tame our fear by pushing away our thoughts of our own demise, allowing us a temporary respite until another closer encounter with the Pale Horse.

We are good at denying the most certain thing we have: our mortality. We accept different religions and beliefs, but we can't accept our finitude. We dread the news from doctors and seek multiple professional opinions in case the diagnosis we receive is disappointing. "*Why me?*"

We put off writing our wills and make plans for three lifetimes ahead. "*I can't die, not yet.*" Our mortality is veiled beneath a thousand tasks, problems, and emotions that keep us feeling alive. And that's for the better: acting and planning increase our chances of survival while existential questioning only sinks us into a state of dread.

Yet, alienation from the reality of our mortality can be detrimental. It leads to engaging in risky behaviors, such as drinking and driving, as well as the less alarming but nonetheless pernicious ones, such as working at a job we despise. You might think the second example doesn't conceal much harm, that boo-hoo, the majority work jobs they'd rather not. Besides,

INFINITY ON OUR FINITUDE, OR MEMENTO MORI

you have a plan: you will endure a few years of unpleasant work to reach a desirable X. But that assumes you still have a few decades ahead of you, let alone a few years, which even being a case still doesn't guarantee that the desirable X will be achieved. And here's what's definitely happening: your time on this planet is decreasing. During every working hour. During every waking and sleeping moment. With this perspective in mind, what seemed like a sensible idea — *"just one more year of this draining drudgery"* — may turn out to be your greatest regret — *"if only I had stopped that nonsense earlier."* The anguish coming from regrets of irreversible waste can poison the remaining years of your life. Isn't it one of the worst emotional pains we can experience — the hopelessness of the inability to change the past, and therefore having to put up with the painful present?

A dull or absent sense of our mortality makes us more compliant — we're more likely to say "yes" and devote our finite resources to what we will later regret. But if we keep in mind that we only have a limited amount of time, our decisions will be more sensible and satisfying, leading to a happier life.

Forgetting our finitude has another hazard to our well-being: we put off our dreams. Sometimes it makes sense — if we don't have an extra $5,000, we shouldn't go on vacation to the Maldives now since it will neither benefit our bank account nor our conscience. But when reasons for our delays are psychological rather than tangible — we can travel to a desirable destination but for a number of fears and misconceptions we don't — we drive ourselves into a hole of discontent in which our lives turn into a broken record of sorrow. We say *later, later,* until *later* becomes *too late* and all we can think of is *if only*. As temporary residents of a town who think that they'll have plenty of time to visit a local landmark or a restaurant, only to leave the town later and never come back, regretting the missed opportunity.

We are all guests in this town of Life. There are no guarantees that we'll visit the places we want and do this and that, so sometimes evoking a possibility that we may actually cease to exist — one year from now, or even tomorrow — can help us to better calibrate our life compass.

Despite our best efforts, we can never be sure we'll achieve our goals. We may get off at the halfway point of a project, early in our family life, or even before we begin a meaningful endeavor. We may stop existing without ever having experienced what love is, learned what we are capable of, and understood what happiness is. That's why it's crucial to remember this: our life on this Earth is limited and what we have now may be all we'll ever have.

Think about what you would regret most if you were to die tomorrow. Rather than dismissing this scenario as hypothetical, take a moment to see that it's not that impossible. More than 180,000 people die every day. And while this number primarily consists of deaths of the elderly and the severely ill, a proportion of deaths fall under the category of "accidental", from the word "accident", an unexpected event. Considering

INFINITY ON OUR FINITUDE, OR MEMENTO MORI

the possibility of your death, what would you change? What would you say "yes" to and what would you say "no" to? Actions that fall into the first category give meaning to your existence; actions under the second category drain your energy and postpone your fulfillment. This exercise, a reminder of your ephemerality, will help you get your priorities right and balance them with your grandiose plans.

We never know when the end will come, but having a source of fulfillment each day makes such a prospect less terrifying. As long as we are guided by our values, we end up on the right path no matter where we are on the journey. That's a life well lived.

The knowledge that we are not eternal, along with everything we have, helps us truly dive into our life, find joy in its simple pleasures and appreciate its even challenging times. Only by understanding that our abilities to feel, think, and act won't last and that the day will come when things will change for us (vanish entirely or morph into something unknown) can we give them the true value they deserve.

Embrace and cherish your one and only Life.

> *To die is poignantly bitter, but the idea of having to die without having lived is unbearable.*
>
> Erich Fromm

WRITE DOWN

what you would do today if tomorrow never came:

_____

_____

_____

If today were your last day, how would you describe yourself and the life you've lived?

_____

_____

_____

_____

_____

INFINITY ON OUR FINITUDE, OR MEMENTO MORI

_____

_____

_____

_____

_____

Does reflecting on your life bring you peace or unrest? If it's the latter, try identifying areas where you may be sabotaging yourself and preventing yourself from living the life you want. Consider revisiting the book and completing all the exercises to gain better clarity on your beliefs, values, and goals.

Remember, as long as you are breathing and thinking, it's never too late to align your life with your values. Doing so can make your life more meaningful and enjoyable. Go for it!

INSTEAD OF AN AFTERWORD

INSTEAD OF AN AFTERWORD

No amount of reading books, listening to podcasts, or watching videos can substitute for firsthand experiences. It is through making choices, experimenting, and learning from these experiences that we grow wiser and better equipped to live a fulfilling life.

I hope this collection has guided you in refining your direction, recognizing your vulnerabilities, and valuing your strengths. My sincerest wish is that you will revisit this book and continue to engage in insightful debates with yourself, or with me. You are more than welcome to comment on my new essays on my Medium blog[1], or to reach out to me directly via email[2].

NOTES

ATTENDING ATTENTION

1. "Information Theory - Physiology." Encyclopædia Britannica. https://www.britannica.com/science/information-theory/Physiology (accessed April 5, 2023).

RESOLVING CONTRADICTIONS

1. *Honesty before glory.*

JUDGING PREJUDGEMENTS

1. *A great illustration of why we make poor predictions about the future can be found in Dr. Gilbert's book Stumbling on Happiness: Part IV.*

UNBORING BOREDOM

1. Danckert, James, and John D. Eastwood. Out of My Skull: The Psychology of Boredom. Cambridge, MA: Harvard University Press, 2020. https://www.hup.harvard.edu/catalog.php?isbn=9780674984677&content=bios.
2. Motivation and Emotion. New York, NY: Springer. https://www.springer.com/journal/11031.
3. Goetz, Thomas, Anne C. Frenzel, Nathan C. Hall, Ulrike E. Nett, Reinhard Pekrun, and Anastasiya A. Lipnevich. "Types of Boredom: An Experience Sampling Approach." Motivation and Emotion 38, no. 3(2014):401-419.doi:10.1007/s11031-013-9385-y.AccessedApril 5, 2023. https://link.springer.com/article/10.1007/s11031-013-9385-y.

4. Martin Heidegger (1889 – 1976) — a German philosopher, best known for his contributions to philosophy, particularly for his ideas on existentialism, ontology, and being and time and infamously known for being a difficult philosopher, as his writing style and philosophical ideas can be complex and abstract.
5. Heidegger, Martin. The Fundamental Concepts of Metaphysics: World, Finitude, Solitude. Bloomington, IN: Indiana University Press, 1995.
6. Mann, Sandi, and Rebekah Cadman. "Does being bored make us more creative?" Creativity Research Journal 26, no. 2 (2014): 165-173. doi:10.1080/10400419.2014.901073. Link: https://www.tandfonline.com/doi/abs/10.1080/10400419.2014.901073
7. I'm aware that such distilling of the aspects of Heidegger's types of boredom can be misleading. And it's likely that science, including psychology, philosophy, and social studies, will develop more nuanced views of boredom, breaking it down into multiple categories with more profound differentiation in the future. As for this article, I will focus on what we all know firsthand — the everyday experience of "Doh! It's boring! Please make it stop." It can worsen our lives if we succumb to it.
8. Nardi, William R., Joel W. Hughes, David M. Fresco, Jeffrey M. Greeson, Richard Josephson, and John F. Thayer. "Mindfulness and Cardiovascular Health: Qualitative Findings on Mechanisms from the Mindfulness-based Blood Pressure Reduction (MB-BP) Study." PLoS ONE 15, no. 9 (2020): e0239533. doi:10.1371/journal.pone.0239533. Accessed April 5, 2023. https://www.ncbi.nlm.nih.gov/pmc/articles/PMC7510988/.
9. Nesvold, Anders, Morten W. Fagerland, Svend Davanger, Øyvind Ellingsen, Erik E. Solberg, Are Holen, Knut Sevre, and Dan Atar. "Increased Heart Rate Variability During Nondirective Meditation." European Journal of Preventive Cardiology 19, no. 4 (2012): 773-780. doi:10.1177/1741826711414625. Accessed April 5, 2023. https://pubmed.ncbi.nlm.nih.gov/21693507/.

10. The trick to conquering boredom while studying is to find a balance between "it's too easy to understand, there's nothing new and so I'm bored" and "it's too difficult, I don't get anything and so I'm bored." That's where awareness and self-control come in. Don't get discouraged too quickly too easily, don't under/overvalue the knowledge you accumulate; be attentive and open to learning. Then boredom won't be an issue. The headache of deep thinking might be, though.

ACCEPTING REJECTION

1. Romeo, Russell D. "The Teenage Brain: The Stress Response and the Adolescent Brain." Current Directions in Psychological Science 22, no. 2 (2013): 140-145. doi:10.1177/0963721413475445. Accessed April 5, 2023.
https://www.ncbi.nlm.nih.gov/pmc/articles/PMC4274618/.

INFINITY ON OUR FINITUDE, OR MEMENTO MORI

1. "The Arzamas Horror" refers to an episode of extreme fear and confusion that Leo Tolstoy experienced in the city of Arzamas. This experience led him to confront his fear of death, and he documented his thoughts and emotions in the diary entry "Diary of a Lunatic," which was published in 1884.

INSTEAD OF AN AFTERWORD

1. https://medium.com/@anastasiawhy
2. contact@anastasiawhy.com

ABOUT THE AUTHOR

Anastasia Petrenko is a dynamic entrepreneur and writer, originally from Ukraine and now dividing her time between Canada and Costa Rica.

With a passion for asking tough questions and challenging common beliefs, Anastasia regularly contributes to Medium, sharing her unique perspective with a growing audience.

In addition to her non-fiction writing, Anastasia is currently working on her debut novel while sipping on hot tea next to her electronics.

www.ingramcontent.com/pod-product-compliance
Lightning Source LLC
Chambersburg PA
CBHW071223080526
44587CB00013BA/1482